Literature & Thought

Echoes from Mt. Olympus

Perfection Learning®

EDITORIAL DIRECTOR   Julie A. Schumacher, Carol Francis

SENIOR EDITOR   Terry Ofner

EDITORS   Rebecca Christian
Linda Mazunik

PERMISSIONS   The Permissions Group, Glenview, IL

REVIEWERS   Mary Gershon
Lynne Albright
Ann Tharnish

DESIGN AND PHOTO RESEARCH
Jan Michalson
Lisa Lorimor

IMAGE PRODUCTION   Jane Wonderlin

COVER ART PORTRAIT OF HERMES 1992 Valerii Koshliakov
The Christian Keesee Collection, Oklahoma City, OK

ACKNOWLEDGMENTS

"Apollo and Artemis: The Twins." Reprinted with the permission of Atheneum Books for Young Readers, and imprint of Simon & Schuster Children's Publishing Division from *Greek Myths: Gods, Heroes and Monsters* by Ellen Switzer and Costas. Text copyright © 1988 Ellen Switzer and Costas.

"Arachne" from *Greek Myths*. Copyright © 1949, renewed 1977 by Olivia E. Coolidge. Reprinted by permission of Houghton Mifflin Co. All rights reserved.

"Artemis, Orion and the Seven Sisters" from *The Faber Book of Greek Legends*, edited by Kathleen Lines, Faber and Faber, Ltd., 1973. Reprinted by permission.

"Big Baby: Hermes." Reprinted with the permission of Margaret K. McElderry Books, an imprint of Simon & Schuster Children's Publishing Division from *Greek Gods and Goddesses* by Geraldine McCaughrean. Text copyright © 1997 Geraldine McCaughrean. Also from *The Orchard Book of Greek Gods and Goddesses* by Geraldine McCaughrean first published in the UK by Orchard Books in 1997, a division of The Watts Publishing Group Limited, 96 Leonard Street, London EC2A 4XD.

"Cupid and Psyche" from *Greek Myths, Western Style: Toga Tales with an Attitude*, by Barbara McBride-Smith. © 1998 by Barbara McBride-Smith. Reprinted by permission of Marian Reiner.

CONTINUED ON PAGE 160

WHY DOES MYTH ENDURE?

The question above is the *essential question* that you will consider as you read this book. The literature, activities, and organization of the book will lead you to think critically about this question and to develop a deeper understanding of mythology.

To help you shape your answer to the broad essential question, you will read and respond to four sections, or clusters of literature. Each cluster addresses a specific question and thinking skill.

CLUSTER ONE What are the qualities of the gods and goddesses?
GENERALIZE

CLUSTER TWO How does myth explain nature?
COMPARE AND CONTRAST

CLUSTER THREE How does myth explain human nature? **EVALUATE**

CLUSTER FOUR Thinking on your own **SYNTHESIZE**

Notice that the final cluster asks you to think independently about your answer to the essential question—*Why does myth endure?*

Echoes from Mt. Olympus

Hail, children of Zeus! Tell of the everlasting gods. Tell how, in the beginning, gods and earth came to be, and rivers, and the boundless sea with its raging swell, and the gleaming stars, and the wide heaven above, and the gods who were born of them, givers of good things; and how those gods divided their dignities, and also how at the first they took Olympus.

from the *Theogony*

Table of Contents

CLUSTER FOUR   Thinking on Your Own   101

Thinking Skill   SYNTHESIZING

The All-Too-Human Gods

There is a lot of talk these days about dysfunctional families. These are families that simply don't work, that are troubled in one way or the other. They do more harm than good, we are told, and they are a blight on our time. From all the hype about families lately, one might think they are a fairly new thing.

But dysfunctional families have been around for a long time. In fact, in the days of ancient Greece and Rome, the universe itself was said to have been run by one of the most troubled families ever. The gods who lived on Mt. Olympus, that fabled peak in northern Greece, were a family counselor's worst nightmare.

Consider Zeus, the god of lightning and the ruler of the heavens. He was the head of the family, and he ruled wisely in some matters. But he was also an unfaithful husband who fathered numerous children by women he never married—and sometimes never saw again.

His wife, Hera (who was also his sister, by the way), was understandably jealous. No one can blame her for punishing her husband whenever she could. Unfortunately, she was also cruel to his unwitting mortal lovers. And she made life miserable for those children, including the hero Hercules and the vine god Dionysus.

Few of the other gods were models of good behavior. Hermes, the messenger god, was sometimes a thief. Aphrodite, the goddess of love, was unhappily married to the lame god of the forge, Hephaestus. So she had a sordid fling with Ares, the god of war.

When Hades, the ruler of the dead, decided to take a wife, he seized the young goddess Persephone by force. The grief of Persephone's mother, Demeter, brought winter to the world and almost destroyed humankind.

Indeed, trouble often came to men and women when the gods misbehaved. Like Zeus, the god Apollo sometimes ruined the lives of mortal lovers. And when a

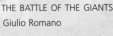

THE BATTLE OF THE GIANTS
Giulio Romano

9

hunter accidentally saw the goddess Artemis bathing, she had him torn to pieces by his own dogs. Likewise, when gods like Athena and Poseidon were unhappy, war and destruction actually broke out in the world.

The only Olympian deity who did no harm was Hestia, the kindly goddess of the hearth. Is it any surprise that there are no interesting stories told about her?

And what of the people who worshipped these troublesome gods? Interestingly, both the ancient Greeks and Romans rose to great heights of civilization and culture.

During the fifth century B.C., the city of Athens became the most powerful city-state in Greece. It achieved great things in sculpture, architecture, drama, and philosophy. It even produced the world's first experiment in democratic government.

Today, this "Golden Age" of Athens is regarded as one of the high points of civilization. And yet Athens' citizens never gave up their reverence for the often ill-behaved Olympian gods.

Eventually, Rome replaced Greece as the center of civilization. Not the most original people in the world, the Romans adopted the Olympian gods as their own. They did, however, change most of the deities' names. For

example, Zeus became Jove, and Hera became Juno. In this book, you may notice inconsistencies in the spelling of names and even in facts from tale to tale. This is the result of many tellers telling many tales over many years.

By 27 B.C., the Romans ruled the greatest empire in the ancient world. During the following two centuries, the world was largely without war. This era was known as the *Pax Romana,* or "Roman Peace." The cultural achievements of Rome came to rival those of Athens. And yet, like the Greeks before them, the Romans honored the unruly Olympians.

What all these great civilizations had in common is that they revered what we would now call a dysfunctional family. Why? Perhaps they saw something of their own faults and frailties in the Olympian deities. For even at their heights, the Greek and Roman civilizations were far from perfect. The Athenian Golden Age was marred by frequent wars, and the *Pax Romana* was an age of dictatorial emperors. Moreover, both Greeks and Romans kept slaves and treated women poorly.

For all their greatness, the Greeks and Romans may have learned humility from their gods. And although we no longer believe in the Olympians today, perhaps they can teach us a similar lesson. We are, after all, only human— much like the gods themselves.

11

Gallery of Gods and Goddesses

Zeus

GREEK NAME: Zeus

ROMAN NAME: Jupiter, Jove

JOB DESCRIPTION: king of all gods; god of heavens and earth; ruler of weather and giver of justice

SYMBOLS AND EMBLEMS: thunderbolt, eagle, woodpecker, oak tree

Hera

GREEK NAME: Hera

ROMAN NAME: Juno

JOB DESCRIPTION: queen of the gods; goddess of marriage and childbirth

SYMBOLS AND EMBLEMS: cow, peacock, lion

Poseidon

GREEK NAME: Poseidon

ROMAN NAME: Neptune

JOB DESCRIPTION: god of the sea and earthquakes

SYMBOLS AND EMBLEMS: trident, dolphin, horse, bull

Demeter

GREEK NAME: Demeter

ROMAN NAME: Ceres

JOB DESCRIPTION: goddess of earth, agriculture, and fertility

SYMBOLS AND EMBLEMS: sheaf of wheat, cornucopia, poppy flower

Hephaestus

GREEK NAME: Hephaestus

ROMAN NAME: Vulcan

JOB DESCRIPTION: god of fire, craftsmen, and metalworkers

SYMBOLS AND EMBLEMS: quail

Athena

GREEK NAME: Athena/Athene

ROMAN NAME: Minerva

JOB DESCRIPTION: goddess of wisdom, courage, and war

SYMBOLS AND EMBLEMS: owl, olive tree, Medusa-head shield

Aphrodite

GREEK NAME: Aphrodite

ROMAN NAME: Venus

JOB DESCRIPTION: goddess of love and beauty

SYMBOLS AND EMBLEMS: dove, sparrow, seagull, rose, and myrtle shrub

Ares

GREEK NAME: Ares

ROMAN NAME: Mars

JOB DESCRIPTION: god of war, hatred, and violence

SYMBOLS AND EMBLEMS: dog, vulture, wild boar, and bloodstained spear

Apollo

GREEK NAME: Apollo

ROMAN NAME: Apollo

JOB DESCRIPTION: god of sunlight, prophecy, medicine, archery, poetry, music, and unmarried men

SYMBOLS AND EMBLEMS: laurel wreath, mouse, golden chariot, golden lyre, golden bow and arrows

Artemis

GREEK NAME: Artemis

ROMAN NAME: Diana

JOB DESCRIPTION: goddess of moon, hunting, and unmarried women

SYMBOLS AND EMBLEMS: she-bear, deer, silver chariot, silver bow and arrows, crescent-moon crown

Hermes

GREEK NAME: Hermes

ROMAN NAME: Mercury

JOB DESCRIPTION: god of trade, travel, and theft; messenger of gods; conductor of souls to underworld

SYMBOLS AND EMBLEMS: winged headband and winged sandals, staff with two snakes twined around it, crane

Dionysus

GREEK NAME: Dionysus

ROMAN NAME: Bacchus

JOB DESCRIPTION: god of wine, parties, and drama

SYMBOLS AND EMBLEMS: ivy, vine, grape bunches, wine cup, leopard

Myth into Language

The characters and events of the myths have given birth to words and phrases we use everyday. The words below are descendants of classic mythology. (Asterisks indicate the gods' and goddesses' Roman names; all others are Greek.)

Achilles heel is a symbol of weakness. The expression comes from Achilles, a warrior who died when a poisoned arrow pierced his heel. It was the only part of his body that was vulnerable.

Adonis is a term for a strikingly handsome man. Adonis was a handsome hunter who was pursued by Aphrodite, the goddess of love.

Ambrosia is a dessert made of oranges and coconut. Ambrosia was the food of the gods.

Aphrodisiac means love potion. It is derived from Aphrodite, who was the goddess of love.

Apollo is the name for several space vehicles. Apollo was god of the sun and patron of the sciences.

Arachnid is a scientific term for a class of invertebrate animals, including spiders. It comes from the story of Arachne, a mortal who was turned into a spider by the goddess Athena. (A related word is *arachnophobia*.)

Atlas is a collection of maps. Atlas was a giant who unsuccessfully fought Zeus, the king of the gods. He was punished by being forced to hold up the sky.

Cereal is named for Ceres,* goddess of the harvest.

Chaos means disorder. Chaos was the father of all gods. He imposed order on the swirling winds and waters at the beginning of creation. (A related word is *chaotic*.)

Chronology is the science that deals with measuring time. It comes from Cronos, the father of the gods, who was known as Father Time. (Related words are *chronic* and *chronicle*.)

Cloth comes from Clotho, one of The Three Fates (see *fate* below). Clotho spun the thread of life on her spindle.

Cupidity means intense desire. It is named after Cupid,* who was the god of love. The chubby angel with a bow and arrow is familiar to us from Valentine's Day cards, but the Cupid of myth was depicted as an adult.

Echo is a word for the repetition of a sound. Echo talked so much that the gods punished her by allowing her only to repeat what others say.

Fate means destiny. The Three Fates decided how long a person's life would be at birth by snipping a thread that measured years in feet and months in inches.(Related words are *fatal, fatalism,* and *fatality*.)

Flora is a scientific term for plant life. It comes from Flora,* the goddess of flowering plants. (Related words are *floral* and *florist*.)

Fortune, or luck, is named for Fortuna.* This goddess spun a wheel to decide how to distribute fortune to mortals. (A related word is *fortunately*.)

Fury means rage. The Furies punished evildoers in the underworld. (Related words are *furious* and *furor*.)

Grace is a word for charm. A trio of sister goddesses, The Graces, were in charge of dispensing beauty and charm. (Related words are *graceful* and *gracious*.)

Herculean task is a job involving great effort. Hercules was the muscle-bound hero who rose to the challenge of 12 seemingly impossible labors imposed on him by Hera, queen of the gods.

Hypnosis is a state resembling sleep in which a person easily accepts suggestions on what to say or do. Hypnos was the god of sleep. (Related words are *hypnotic*, *hypnotism*, and *hypnotist*.)

January is named for Janus,* the god of beginnings and endings.

Jovial means hearty and friendly. It comes from Jove,* who was king of the gods. He was healthy and happy because he was born under a lucky planet. Jupiter* (see below) is another name for Jove.

June is named for Juno,* the goddess of marriage and childbirth.

Jupiter, the planet, is named after Jupiter.* He was king of the gods and in charge of light, the sky, and weather.

Mars, the planet, is named for Mars.* He was the god of war. (Related words are *Martian*, *martial*, and *martial arts*.)

Mercury is the name of both the planet and the element. Mercury* was the speedy messenger of the gods. (A related word is *mercurial*.)

Muse is a word that means to wonder, marvel, or reflect. The Nine Muses inspired the fine arts. (Related words are *amuse*, *music*, and *musical*.)

Narcissism means excessive love of oneself. Narcissus was so enchanted by his own reflection in water that he couldn't look away. The gods turned him into the flower called narcissus.

Neptune, the planet, is named for Neptune.* He was a god of the sea.

Ocean is derived from Oceanus, a lord of the seas. He was one of the giants who unsuccessfully battled against Zeus. (Related words are *oceanfront*, *oceangoing*, and *oceanic*.)

Odyssey is an adventurous journey. It takes its name from Odysseus, the hero who sailed the Greek isles having one hair-raising adventure after another.

Olive branches were given by the Greeks after battle as a symbol of peacemaking; today the expression "extending the olive branch" means attempting to make peace.

The Olympic Games are famous worldwide games named for athletic contests held on Mt. Olympus. (A related word is *Olympian*.)

Oracle is a person who gives wise opinions and decisions. Oracle answered questions about the will of the gods. (A related word is *oracular*.)

Owls came to be symbols of wisdom because Athena, the goddess of wisdom, was often pictured with an owl perched on her shoulder.

Panic means sudden, intense fright. Part god and part goat, Pan lived in the woods. There his bloodcurdling war cry made soldiers flee in terror.

Pluto, the planet, is named for Pluto. He was god of the underworld, or land of the dead. Hades is not only another name for Pluto, but also a word for the underworld itself.

Psyche is the soul and mind. Psyche gained self-knowledge while performing difficult tasks. (Related words are *psychiatry* and *psychology*.)

Tantalize means tempt. Tantalus was a Greek king who so angered the gods that when he went to Hades, they tortured him by keeping food and drink always slightly out of his reach.

Titans is a name used by several sports teams. It comes from giants called the Titans. Perhaps the teams don't realize that when the Titans waged war against Zeus, they lost. And of course the huge ship, Titanic, sunk after hitting an iceberg.

Typhoon is a tropical cyclone. It gets its name from Typhon, a monster who flew through the air spewing flames and shrieking.

Uranus, the planet, is named for Uranus. God of the sky and father of the Titans, he also gives a variation of his name to the element uranium.

Venus, the planet, is named for Venus.* She was the goddess of love.

Volcanoes are named for Vulcan, the god of fire.

CLUSTER ONE

What Are the Qualities of the Gods and Goddesses?
Thinking Skill   GENERALIZING

Zeus and Hera

BERNARD EVSLIN
DOROTHY EVSLIN
NED HOOPES

Cronos, father of the gods, who gave his name to time, married his sister Rhea, goddess of earth. Now, Cronos had become king of the gods by killing his father Oranos, the First One, and the dying Oranos had prophesied, saying, "You murder me now, and steal my throne—but one of your own sons will dethrone you, for crime begets crime."

So Cronos was very careful. One by one, he swallowed his children as they were born: First, three daughters—Hestia, Demeter, and Hera; then two sons—Hades and Poseidon. One by one, he swallowed them all.

Rhea was furious. She was determined that he should not eat her next child who she felt sure would be a son. When her time came, she crept down the slope of Olympus to a dark place to have her baby. It was a son, and she named him Zeus. She hung a golden cradle from the branches of an olive tree, and put him to sleep there. Then she went back to the top of the mountain. She took a rock and wrapped it in swaddling clothes and held it to her breast, humming a lullaby. Cronos came snorting and bellowing out of his great bed, snatched the bundle from her, and swallowed it, clothes and all.

Rhea stole down the mountainside to the swinging golden cradle, and took her son down into the fields. She gave him to a shepherd family to raise, promising that their sheep would never be eaten by wolves.

Here Zeus grew to be a beautiful young boy, and Cronos, his father, knew nothing about him. Finally, however, Rhea became lonely for him and brought him back to the court of the gods, introducing him to Cronos as the new cupbearer.[1] Cronos was pleased because the boy was beautiful.

One night Rhea and Zeus prepared a special drink. They mixed mustard and salt with the nectar.[2] Next morning, after a mighty swallow, Cronos vomited up first a stone, and then Hestia, Demeter, Hera, Hades, and Poseidon—who, being gods, were still undigested, still alive. They thanked Zeus, and immediately chose him to be their leader.

Then a mighty battle raged. Cronos was joined by the Titans, his half-brothers, huge, twisted, dark creatures taller than trees, whom he kept pent up in the mountains until there was fighting to be done. They attacked the young gods furiously. But Zeus had allies too. He had gone to darker caverns—caves under caves under caves, deep in the mountainside—formed by the first bubbles of the cooling earth. Here, Cronos, thousands of centuries before (a short time in the life of a god) had pent up other monsters, the one-eyed Cyclopes, and the Hundred-handed Ones. Zeus unshackled these ugly cousins and led them against the Titans.

There was a great rushing and tumult in the skies. The people on earth heard mighty thunder, and saw mountains shatter. The earth quaked and tidal waves rolled as the gods fought. The Titans were tall as trees, and old Cronos was a crafty leader. He attacked fiercely, driving the young gods before him. But Zeus had laid a trap. Halfway up the slope of Olympus, he whistled for his cousins, the Hundred-handed Ones, who had been lying in ambush. They took up huge boulders, a hundred each, and hurled them downhill at the Titans. The Titans thought the mountain itself was falling on them. They broke ranks, and fled.

The young goat-god Pan was shouting with joy. Later he said that it was his shout that made the Titans flee. That is where we get the word "panic."

Now the young gods climbed to Olympus, took over the castle, and Zeus became their king. No one knows what happened to Cronos and his Titans. But sometimes mountains still explode in fire, and the earth still quakes, and no one knows exactly why.

One story says that Zeus killed Cronos with a scythe[3] —the same one that Cronos had used on Oranos. Perhaps this is the real meaning behind the greeting-card pictures we exchange on New Year's Day, a rosy little baby confronting an old man who carries a scythe. Memories of the old gods crop up in odd places.

1 **cupbearer:** person who fills and serves cups of wine

2 **nectar:** sweet drink of the gods

3 **scythe:** long, curved blade used for cutting grain

Now, these gods reigned for some three thousand years. There were many of them, but twelve chief ones. Zeus married his sister Hera—a family habit. They were always quarreling. He angered her by his infidelities; she enraged him with her suspicions. She was the queen of intriguers and always found it easy to outwit Zeus, who was busy with many things.

Once she persuaded the other gods into a plot against him. She drugged his drink; they surrounded him as he slept and bound him with rawhide thongs.[4] He raged and roared and swore to destroy them, but they had stolen his thunderbolt, and he could not break the thongs.

But his faithful cousin, the Hundred-handed Briareus, who had helped him against the Titans, was working as his gardener. He heard the quarreling under the palace window, looked in, and saw his master bound to the couch. He reached through with his hundred long arms and unbound the hundred knots.

Zeus jumped from the couch and seized his thunderbolt. The terrified plotters fell to their knees, weeping and pleading. He seized Hera and hung her in the sky, binding her with golden chains. And the others did not dare to rescue her, although her voice was like the wind sobbing. But her weeping kept Zeus awake. In the morning he said he would free her if she swore never to rebel again. She promised, and Zeus promised to mend his ways too. But they kept watching each other.

Zeus was king of the gods, lord of the sky. His sister Demeter was the earth-goddess, lady of growing things. His sister Hera, queen of the gods, was also his wife. His brother Poseidon was god of the sea. His other brother, Hades, ruled a dark domain, the underworld, the land beyond death.

The other gods in the Pantheon were Zeus's children; three of them were also Hera's. These were Ares, the god of war; Hephaestus, the smith-god, forger of weapons; and Eris, goddess of discord, who shrieks beside Ares in his battle chariot. [Athene, goddess of wisdom, sprang from Zeus's head.] The rest of Zeus's children were born out of wedlock. Three of them entered the Pantheon. [They were Hermes and the twins Apollo and Artemis.] ∾

---

4 **rawhide thongs:** leather strips

The Firebringer

Louis Untermeyer

The long war between the fearful Titans and the Olympian gods had finally come to an end with the defeat of the Titans. Zeus, leader of the gods, established his rule in heaven and imprisoned his enemies in Tartarus, a dark domain under the earth.

Not all the Titans had fought against the Olympians. One of those who had helped Zeus was Prometheus, on whom Zeus decided to bestow his favor.

"I have made men and women, three races of them," he told Prometheus. "They did not please me. One race did nothing but eat and drink; another planned only evil things; the third fought among themselves, had no reverence for the gods, and no respect for anything. Nevertheless, mankind should have one more chance, and this time it will be you, not I, who will make a new race. Make men and women out of clay, mix in any other element they may need, and let them work out their destiny. Use any material that is on earth. But one thing you must not do. You must not take anything from the heavens, nothing that belongs to the immortal gods. If you do, there will be a punishment too terrible to contemplate."

Prometheus obeyed. He scooped up some wet clay, and began to shape creatures resembling the gods. In their bodies he built characteristics of all the animals: the pride of the lion, the cleverness of the fox, the loyalty of the dog, the bravery of the bull. He gave them knowledge as well as instinct so they would know how to plow a field, plant seed, cultivate a crop, and reap a harvest. He taught them how to tame wild

PROMETHEUS CARRYING FIRE
Jan Cossiers

things, shear sheep, and milk cows. He showed them how to make tools out of stone and how to make weapons to protect themselves from the horns of deer and other beasts. He instructed them how to exist in the wilderness, how to erect shelters and eventually, how to build houses.

But they were not happy. They shivered miserably through the winters; they sickened on uncooked food; they could not bake bread, bend cold iron, or melt metal. One thing was needed, and that one thing was forbidden: fire, the heavenly fire that belonged to the gods. For a while Prometheus hesitated. He remembered Zeus's threat and realized that anyone who took anything that belonged to the gods would suffer terribly. But men needed the gift of fire; they needed it not only for comfort but also for their future.

Prometheus knew what he had to do and how to do it. He took a long hollow reed, dried it, and filled the inside with pith.[1] He walked in and out of Olympus; none of the gods noticed what he was doing. He touched the gods' hearth-fire with his reed that looked like a walking stick, and a spark from the hearth caught on the pith which burned slowly like the wick of a candle. He brought this from Olympus, lit the first flame on earth, and taught men how to kindle fire whenever it was needed for warmth or for work, for cooking food, shaping metal tools, or creating things of beauty.

When Zeus saw smoke arising, he was furious. He thundered at Prometheus. "I warned you!" he stormed. "Because you dared to bring the gods' fire down to the earthlings you love so much, you shall never leave the earth again. You shall be chained to a rock on the highest peak of the bleak Caucasus.[2] There you shall lie exposed to the heavens you violated. You shall be burned by the rays of the fiery sun and frozen by the icy winds of winter. You shall lie there sleepless and helpless, for no power will come to free you and no creature will hear you. Every day an eagle will tear your flesh and feed upon your liver, and every night the wound will heal so that the eagle can prey upon you again and again."

Prometheus was bound, fettered to the rock with chains of iron and manacles of brass. Years passed, the tortures continued, and Prometheus bore the cruelty of Zeus. He never cried out his agony nor did he regret what he had done. From time to time Zeus sent a messenger to urge

---

1 **pith:** spongy plant tissue from the center of the stem

2 **Caucasus:** mountain range between the Black Sea and the Caspian Sea; considered the boundary between Europe and Asia

Prometheus to repent. Prometheus refused. Then said the messenger, "Zeus knows that you have some secret knowledge about the fate of the gods. If you will disclose the secret, Zeus will set you free."

Prometheus knew that one day Zeus would be dethroned by a son of his own, just as Zeus had overthrown his father. Prometheus knew who the mother would be, and Zeus needed to know the name of the mortal woman so he could guard against her offspring. But Prometheus refused to talk. He remained inflexible, suffering indescribable pain rather than help a tyrant who would not help mankind.

Finally he was freed, not by Zeus, but by Herakles—the Romans called him Hercules—who shot the eagle and restored Prometheus to liberty. Then he went back to work among men.

It was Prometheus (according to the ancients) who gave man humanity. From the Firebringer, mankind inherited his forethought, his fearless spirit as a fighter against tyranny, his courage and, most of all, his compassion for all people everywhere. ∾

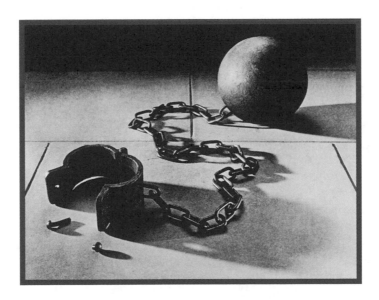

Pandora

BARBARA MCBRIDE-SMITH

Have you ever been making up your bed or fluffing up your pillow, and you came across one of those little tags that reads: UNDER PENALTY OF LAW—DO NOT REMOVE? And you thought to yourself, "Who says? This is my pillow. I can rip this sucker off right now. Are the Pillow Police gonna come in here and arrest me if I do?"

Well, that must have been how Pandora felt about that box. The box had been a wedding present from Papa Zeus. It was a beautiful box, covered with gold and inlaid with jewels. It had a heavy lid held shut by a lock. And underneath that lock there was a tag. It read: UNDER PENALTY OF LAW—DO NOT REMOVE. And Pandora probably said to herself, "Who says? This is *my* box. Papa Zeus gave it to me. Why wouldn't he want me to look inside it?"

You see, Pandora had a problem.

It had all started years and years ago as a feud between Papa Zeus and the Metheus brothers. You remember the Metheus brothers. There was Pro—Prometheus. He was the oldest and the smartest. And then there was Epi—Epimetheus. He wasn't the sharpest knife in the drawer, but he was real proud of his big brother. He used to say, "This here's my bro Pro. He's the brains in the family."

The Metheus boys were Titans, but they lived right alongside the mortals from time to time. They were fond of the mortals and liked to give them presents. That made the mortals worship the ground they walked on. One day Pro decided to give the mortals a present like they had never had before—fire! With fire they could warm their feet and eat cooked meat. The problem was, the only fire that existed was in Papa Zeus's barbecue pit up on Mount Olympus. So one evening while Zeus was out on an affair—of state—Pro slipped in the back gate and stole a red hot coal from the fire pit. He took it down and gave it to the mortals. Well, that made Pro a hero with the mortals, but it chapped ol' Zeus's hide.

And what did Papa Zeus do about it? He punished Prometheus by hanging him on the side of a mountain. Pro hung there all day long in the boiling hot sun. And he hung there all night long in the cold. Then in the wee hours of the morning an eagle flew up to him, sat down on Pro's face, and started to peck at his belly. She pecked and pecked until she plucked his liver plumb out. She swallowed it and took off. Poor ol' Pro had to hang there again all day long in the boiling hot sun and all night long in the cold. He was miserable, shivering, liverless. But he didn't die. He couldn't die because he was immortal. So that night he grew a brand new liver. And the next morning, the eagle was back. She plucked out that new liver, ate it, and took off again. Well, that same old routine went on day after day, month after month, year after year! That liver-loving eagle thought she had a standing invitation for breakfast.

Even after eons of time had gone by, Papa Zeus still wasn't satisfied that the Metheus brothers and their pals, the mortals, had gotten their fair share of punishment for stealing his fire. If there was one thing Zeus was good at, it was revenge. That was when Zeus hit upon the idea of making a *woman*. That's right, the first mortal woman! Up until then the whole world was inhabited by nothing but the good ol' boys. Not a woman amongst them. Not one. How their toilet paper rolls ever got changed is a mystery to me.

Zeus went to his son Phestus, the blacksmith, and asked him to design a creature that would drive the good ol' boys on the earth real crazy. What Phestus built was a woman. He made her strong and he made her beautiful. Zeus made her smart *and* he made her curious. Then Zeus named her Pandora, which means "gift to all."

You getting my drift here? It was a setup right from the start! Papa Zeus gave Pandora that beautiful box, the one covered with gold and inlaid with jewels, the one with the heavy lid and the lock and the little tag. You remember the one: UNDER PENALTY OF LAW—DO NOT REMOVE. Then he sent her off to find Epimetheus and marry up with him. The moment Epi laid eyes on Pandora, he was in love. So they got married. She promised to love, honor, and redecorate. And she got busy straightening out his sock drawer and his life.

For the first couple of weeks, Pandora was so busy being domestic she didn't think much about that box. But when she figured out that house-work was boring, she began to notice that box more and more. She took to dusting it every morning. She polished the jewels every afternoon. One day Epi came home from work early, and when she saw her fondling that box, he shoved it into the closet. "Whoeee, Pandy honey, don't mess with that box! That box is trouble with a capital T and that rhymes with P and that stands for . . . uh . . . for . . ."

"Pooey!" said Pandora. She wasn't scared of that box. She was curious about that box. And she went right on being curious.

As soon as Epi went back to work, she took that box out of the closet and put it on the coffee table. She read the tag under the lock again: UNDER PENALTY OF LAW—DO NOT REMOVE. And she said to herself, "How come I can't open this box? It's *my* box. What could possibly be in here that Papa Zeus wouldn't want me to see?" She commenced to stare at that box for hours each day. Her eyes would glaze over and her jaw would go slack. She'd even talk to that box. She began to look just like a TV soap opera addict. But that box held more troubles than a whole year's worth of "The Bold and the Beautiful," "The Young and the Restless," "All My Children," and "General Hospital" combined. Before long, Pandora was plumb eat up with curiosity. Why couldn't she just remove the lock, lift the lid, and have a tiny peek? She wouldn't take any-thing out of the box and lose it, for crying out loud!

Well, like I said before, Pandora was smart. So she finally figured it out. "Papa Zeus put that sign on the box so that nobody else would mess with it *but* me. After all, it was my present," she thought. "It's a lousy job," she chuckled, "but somebody's gotta do it." She ran out to the garage and got a crowbar. She popped off the lock, lifted up the lid, and . . . well, that's when it all hit the fan!

All the stuff that makes life miserable came jumping out of that box: Sickness, old age, anger, envy, and lust. Racism, sexism, terrorism, and tourism. Communism, and capitalism. Alcoholism, drug addiction, pornography, and censorhip. War and bombs and nuclear waste. Cholesterol, hemorrhoids, PMS and the IRS. Ring-around-the-collar and the heartbreak of psoriasis. Oh yes, all of that stuff and much, much more came flying out of that box.

But there was one little misfit down at the bottom of the box. Her name was Hope. She really didn't want to join the others, but she felt an obligation to take a flying leap. Instead, she took a chance and yelled out, "Pandora! Get a grip, girlfriend! Shut the lid or I'm outta here!"

Just in the nick of time, Pandora got a grip on herself and slammed down the lid and Hope was kept safe in the box.

Under the circumstances, considering she was framed and all, I think Pandora did the best she could for us. You can blame her for your troubles if you want to. People have been giving her a bad rap for thousands of years. But when you're down-and-out and nothing else seems to help, just remember: there's always Hope. She's still there, waiting for you when you need her . . . deep inside. ∾

The Wise Goddess: Athena

BETTY BONHAM LIES

Of all his children, the gray-eyed Athena was Zeus's favorite. She alone was allowed to carry her father's thunderbolt and his great breastplate, called the Aegis. Athena was the only Olympian who was not born of a mother, but sprang directly from the head of Zeus, fully grown and dressed in armor.

Athena was the most complex of the twelve great Olympian gods and goddesses. As the goddess of war, she could perform mighty deeds of battle; at least twice she defeated the war god Ares. Yet war gave her no pleasure. She preferred peace, and would rather settle disputes by wise judgment than by fighting. In this, she was most unlike the wild Ares, who loved battle for its own sake, and was never happier than when he was slaughtering enemies or destroying cities. It was probably Athena's superior intelligence and strategy in battle that made her stronger than the war god with his mindless fury and love of bloodshed. In peacetime, she put off her armor to dress in graceful flowing robes. Although many of the gods desired to marry her, Athena chose to remain single.

Like all of the other deities, Athena took a deep interest in the affairs of mortals. But unlike many of them, she tended to use her power to make life better for those humans she cared for.

This is a typical gesture: Athena competed with Poseidon, the god of the seas, over a new settlement of people, which was destined to be one of the greatest cities in the history of the world. Which of them should become the patron[1] of the city, to be named after the winner? With the other gods and

---

1 **patron:** guardian and protector

PALLAS ATHENA   1898   Franz von Stuck

goddesses sitting as judges, Poseidon and Athena each performed a miraculous act on the heights of Acropolis, overlooking the new city.

First the sea god struck the rock with his trident,[2] and immediately a great fountain of water burst forth. Everyone was amazed: even though the water was salty, it was a wonder to see a spring rising from the top

2 **trident:** a three-pronged spear

of a mountain. Then Athena struck the rock with her spear. From the rocky soil grew a tall olive tree, loaded with fruit. How much more useful that was than a flow of brackish water!

The goddess was made the patroness of the great city, now named Athens in her honor. Ever since that time, the olive tree has been her special tree, and the owl, the symbol of wisdom, her special bird.

It was not only Athens that this goddess protected, but all of civilized life. Think of the innumerable gifts she brought to Earth for the benefit of mortals! She invented the flute and the trumpet for our pleasure, the earthenware bowl for our convenience, and taught all the women's arts, especially weaving. But she also worked to improve farming, inventing the plough[3] and rake, the yoke to harness oxen, and the bridle for horses. She gave us the chariot and the ship; she first taught us the science of mathematics.

During the Trojan War,[4] many of the Olympians took sides; in fact, it was as much a war among the gods and goddesses as between the Greeks and Trojans. Athena took the side of the Greeks, and long after they had won the war, she continued to help them. She watched after Odysseus during his ten-year journey home from the war, offering him advice and assistance when he most needed it. Among her other favorites, to whom she offered help and comfort during their ordeals, were Heracles, Perseus, Jason, Bellerophon, and Orestes and Iphigenia.

Athena, called Minerva by the Romans, was unique among the deities. She defines heroism in a new way: courage does not necessarily mean fighting, but standing firm for what is right. She can serve as a model for women everywhere. The divine protector of human civilization, the goddess of war who preferred peace, the judge who believed in mercy— this was indeed a gracious goddess, and a wise one. ∾

---

3 **plough:** or plow; an instrument used to prepare ground for planting

4 **Trojan War:** a ten-year war between the Greeks and Trojans caused by the kidnapping of Helen of Troy by the Greek warrior Paris

POSEIDON, APOLLO AND ARTEMIS
FROM THE ATHENIAN PARTHENON FRIEZE
447–432 B.C.

Apollo and Artemis: The Twins

ELLEN SWITZER AND COSTAS

One day Zeus saw a beautiful nymph[1] called Leto and fell in love with her. But he noticed that Hera was watching, and so he changed Leto and himself into quails, birds that are brown and speckled and can easily hide in trees and bushes. But Hera was too clever for him. She saw through this disguise immediately and put a curse on Leto. She told the unfortunate nymph that she would be pregnant, and that she would not be able to give birth to her child anywhere the sun could shine.

Then she sent the great serpent Python to enforce her curse, to drive Leto from any sunlit spot. Zeus tried to help the mother of his child and sent the south wind to float her to an island called Delos. It was a small, rocky place, but Python followed anyway. However, because the island was so small, the wind could push it farther out to sea faster than the serpent could swim. And so, finally, Leto had a place where she could give birth.

It turned out that she bore twins. First she had a lovely baby girl she called Artemis. From all the running and hiding, she was so weak that she had difficulty giving birth to her second child. But Artemis, even though she was just a baby, helped her mother, and a beautiful son was born. Leto called him Apollo.

Zeus had a great many children, but none he loved so much as those twins. They were gifted with strength and courage as well as beauty. Apollo had dark gold hair and deep blue eyes, and extraordinary talents in music, poetry, mathematics, and medicine. He became the god of the sun and patron of the arts and sciences.

1 **nymph:** lovely maiden who watches over nature

Of all the gods he was probably the most admirable, in his character as well as in his appearance. He could not tell a lie, and so the oracle,[2] which he established at Delphi,[3] was sought out by Greek kings and commoners alike to find out what the future held for them. When the oracle agreed to speak, it always told the truth, although often the prophecies foretold danger and disaster and generally the actual prophecy was couched in phrases that were hard to interpret and were often misunderstood by those who heard them.

Apollo preached moderation. He told his followers to look into their own hearts to find the beginnings of wisdom. However, like all of the other gods, he sometimes did not practice what he preached. Occasionally he even angered Zeus with his impetuous behavior. When he became jealous or angry, he, too, could be cruel.

As soon as he was old enough to shoot a golden bow and arrow Zeus had given him, Apollo went in search of Python, the serpent who had tortured his mother. He found the serpent at the foot of Mount Parnassus and raced up the mountain to shoot a burning arrow at the animal, which screamed with pain and fled, leaving a trail of blood behind. The serpent's hiding place was the cave of Mother Earth at Delphi, considered a sanctuary (a place where all fighting had to stop) by gods and man alike. Apollo knew that he could not follow the huge snake into the cave, but he breathed on his arrows and created a smoke screen, which he shot into the entrance of the cave. The cave filled with smoke, and the serpent, suffocating from the fumes, had to crawl out. Apollo shot him full of arrows, skinned him, and kept the hide as a souvenir of his revenge.

But he had accomplished his revenge in a sacred place, and Mother Earth complained to Zeus that her sanctuary had been defiled. To make amends, Apollo instituted annual athletic games at Delphi (which really were meant to celebrate his victory), and named them after his enemy: the Pythian Games. He also established the Delphic oracle and named the priestesses who gave advice Pythonesses. This did not help the dead Python, but the gesture appeased Zeus and got Apollo back into his father's good graces.

Like Zeus, Apollo fell in love with and pursued many women. He also had many children. The most famous was his son Aesculapius, who was

2 **oracle:** a place where the future is foretold

3 **Delphi:** a religious center on the southern slope of Mt. Parnassus, located in central Greece

gifted with miraculous medical knowledge. Even today, when physicians take the oath to do their best to heal and not harm their patients, they use the name of Aesculapius as a symbol of medical knowledge and skill.

Aesculapius was the son of Apollo and Coronis, a princess of Thessaly.[4] She was in love with a young mortal, but Apollo carried her off with him. While she was pregnant with Apollo's son, she went back to her old lover. Apollo could not bring himself to kill the mother of his unborn child himself, so he asked his sister, Artemis, to shoot her with one of her arrows.

He wanted to save the child, however, so he delivered the baby (probably one of the first surgical births in history) and turned him over to the god Hermes, who was immediately struck by the infant's extraordinary intelligence.

The child was sent to Chiron, a centaur—half man and half horse—until that time the most gifted physician in Greek mythology. Aesculapius soon improved on his master's methods. He doctored everyone who came to him and was able to heal even those who were on the point of death.

Eventually the young doctor enraged Hades, who went to Zeus to complain that Apollo's son was robbing him of his victims at the very point when they were supposed to cross over from the land of the living to the land of the dead. Zeus picked up his thunderbolt and threw it at Aesculapius and the patient he was curing at the time, sending both to Hades.

Apollo was not only heartbroken, but also very angry. He found a Cyclops[5] who had made his father's thunderbolt and killed him, a sin against Zeus that the ruler of the gods could not allow to go unpunished. So he banished Apollo to Hades forever.

Until this time Leto had kept away from Zeus, realizing that Hera was watching her, and that any attempt to get in touch with her children's father could only bring more misfortune on herself. But the banishment of her beautiful and clever son gave her the courage to go to Zeus and remind him of their old love. Zeus listened to her and relented. Not only did he allow Apollo to come back to Mount Olympus, he even agreed to bring Aesculapius back to life, with a warning not to rob Hades by curing those sick humans who were already on their way across the river Styx.[6]

---

4 **Thessaly:** a region in central Greece bordering the Aegean Sea

5 **Cyclops:** one-eyed giant

6 **Styx:** river through which the living pass on the way to the underworld, or land of the dead

According to one legend, Zeus's reversal of judgment angered Aphrodite. So she ordered Eros to shoot Apollo with the arrow of love, and the mountain nymph, Daphne, who happened to cross his path, with the arrow of indifference. When the beautiful god, not used to being turned down by women, started to follow her, she ran away as fast as she could.

Daphne was the daughter of a river god, and when she realized that Apollo was faster than she, she ran to the river and begged her father to save her. He turned her into a laurel tree.[7] Apollo caught up with the nymph, and found that instead of a beautiful girl, he was hugging a tree with thorns that scratched his face.

So the river god, who knew that Apollo was more powerful than he was and could harm him, gave Apollo a gift to appease him: a crown of laurel leaves. From that day on, crowns of laurel, a plant that would never wither, were awarded to heroes and poets as a sign of extraordinary ability.

Apollo's special friends were the nine Muses, who represented the arts. When he was a very young god, they taught him their skills, so that Apollo became the greatest poet and artist in the universe, improving on everything that the Muses had taught him.

Apollo was one of the few gods who was allowed to keep his original name by the Romans. However, they tended to make him less important than the Greeks had. He was generally pictured as a beautiful young man who somehow never really grew up. Roman statues tend to make him look somehow less masculine than those of the Greeks. His artistic abilities were less respected by the Romans. Music, poetry, and dance were considered among the greatest gifts of the gods by the Greeks, but were generally regarded as entertainment for the masses by the Romans. They respected political and fighting ability in men more than artistic accomplishments.

▲ ▲ ▲

Artemis, Apollo's twin, was, in her own way as beautiful as her brother. While he seemed to be surrounded with a golden light, his sister gleamed like silver. Zeus loved her very much.

On her third birthday, he asked her to make any wish—he would make sure she got what she wanted. Artemis, who, in spite of her youth, had seen all the harm that Aphrodite could do to those over whom she had power, wished that she would always be a young girl—never a woman. She

7 **laurel tree:** an evergreen tree with small green leaves and berries

asked Zeus never to give her to any man. Also, she wished for a silver bow and arrow, the best pack of hounds in the universe, and the freedom to run and hunt over the mountains and in the woods for all eternity.

Zeus granted her wishes. He gave her the gift of eternal chastity, but, considering himself more experienced than his three-year-old daughter, told her that she could change her mind about falling in love at any time, if she got tired of the single life.

Artemis went to Hephaestus and asked him to make her a silver bow, but the god of the forge suggested that silver should be created underwater in a cold light. So Artemis swam to the Cyclops who had made Zeus's thunderbolt, and they fashioned for her the most beautiful silver bow, quiver, and arrows in their power. The quiver had a special magic: As soon as it was empty, it filled up again.

Next she visited Pan, who gave her his ten best dogs. From then on Artemis spent her days and nights hunting deer in the woods and streaking across the sky like a silver bolt. She was worshiped as the goddess of the moon and the stars, chaste but happy and fulfilled. Men who came near her, whether they were gods or humans, were frightened away by her fierce hounds.

In many parts of Greece, young women whose relatives wished to marry them off to men they did not love prayed to Artemis to save them. According to legend, she frequently did, although she sometimes had to turn the girl into a tree, a flower, or a deer. But perhaps the Greeks thought that it was preferable to be turned into an enchanted plant or animal than to have to spend the rest of one's life with a mate one disliked.

The Roman name for Artemis was Diana; she became a favorite subject of sculpture and painting. She is usually seen carrying her bow and accompanied by one or more of her many dogs. ∾

Big Baby Hermes

GERALDINE MCCAUGHREAN

The gods never grow old. Take Hermes. He is seventeen for all eternity, and the other gods never let him forget it. "Fetch this, Hermes. Do that, Hermes. Carry this message. Do as your half brother tells you." He even cooks for them.

But Hermes doesn't mind. He's an easygoing boy. People down on earth ask his protection when they go on journeys: Some of those wild country roads swarm with thieves and ruffians. Mind you, the thieves and ruffians ask the help of Hermes, too. They've probably heard the stories of Hermes's childhood and how light-fingered he was, even as a baby!

The day Hermes was born—in a cave in Arcadia[1]—his mother, Maia, laid him in his cradle and kissed his tufty hair. "Don't cry now. You are a son of Zeus and a secret from his wife. If she hears you are here, Hera will hate you with a deadly hatred, and kill you if she can. So hush, my little Hermes. Don't cry." In rocking the cradle, Maia herself went to sleep.

Hermes was a big baby: big in the morning and much bigger by noon, when he clambered out of his cradle, toddled out of the cave, and met a tortoise. Banging on the tortoise's shell, he heard a throbbing hollow noise he liked. So, emptying out the tortoise, he tied threads of his mother's hair around the shell. When Maia stirred at the pulling of her hair, Hermes plucked a tune that soothed her back to sleep.

---

1 **Arcadia:** or Arcady; a peaceful agricultural region of Greece

Then, slinging his newly invented lyre[2] across his back, Hermes toddled away down the road, making up songs as he went. He was hungry. He wanted a drink of milk.

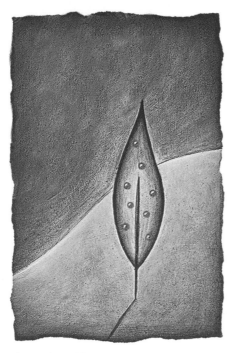

"Watch me go along,
To see what I can find.
Hear me sing my song,
With my lyre tied on behind.
I'm going to find a moo-cow
Maybe one or two cows:
I may just follow
My brother Apollo
And round up quite a few cows!"

All the way to Pieria[3] he walked, growing all the while, and in the middle of the afternoon he found the grazing place of Apollo's shining brown cows. They were all bursting with milk, and Hermes drank all he could drink.

Then, hazel switch[4] in hand, he began to drive the cows back the way he had come. He did not drive them headfirst, but blipped their noses, and made them walk backward, so that the tracks they left would look as if they had been coming, when in fact they had been going. He tied twigs to his feet, as well, to scuff out his own footprints.

Back along the road he toddled, singing as he went, and picking grapes off the vines at the roadside. An old woman tending the vines straightened her aching back to watch him go by. It was a remarkable sight, after all: a baby toddling along in wicker shoes, driving a herd of back-to-front cows.

Hermes put a chubby finger to his lips, as if to say, "Don't breathe a word."

By the time he had hidden the cows—up trees, down holes, under bushes—Maia, his mother, was awake and standing at the door of the

2 **lyre:** a stringed instrument similar to a small harp
3 **Pieria:** a region of Greece
4 **hazel switch:** a flexible twig from the hazel tree used for prodding or whipping

cave. "And where do you think you've been till this time of night?" she demanded, hands on hips.

Hermes climbed into his cradle: It was a bit small for him now—he had grown so much since morning. "Never you mind, Mommy," he said. Then, sucking his thumb, he quickly fell asleep.

When he woke, Apollo was standing over him, shouting till the cave echoed. "Where are my cows?"

"Agoo," said Hermes.

"You don't fool me. Where are my cows, you thieving infant!"

"A-moo?" Hermes said, and chortled.

Apollo's golden hair curled a little tighter. "An old woman saw a baby driving my cows this way. Now get out of bed. I'm taking you before the court of the gods! You can answer to Almighty Zeus for your cattle-rustling!"

▲ ▲ ▲

"Silence in court!" bellowed Zeus as Hermes plucked his tortoise-lyre.

"Answer the charge! Is it true, Hermes, that you stole the cattle of Apollo?"

Hermes stood up. "Almighty gods . . . gentlemen . . . ladies . . . I appeal to you—do I look like a thief? Does it seem to you probable, does it seem to you likely, that I, a little child, a mewling infant, a child of rosy innocence, should walk fifty miles on the day of my birth and carry off—like some vagabond, some deceitful rapscallion—a herd of shining cows?"

"*Yes!*" bawled Apollo.

"Silence in court!"

"And me a vegetarian! A lover of animals! The merest silken butterfly fluttering over my crib is enough to make me laugh aloud at the wondrous beauty of nature!"

"*Shyster!*"[5] shouted Apollo.

"Silence in court!"

Hermes toddled about the courtroom, declaring his innocence, presenting his defense. He laid his baby curls on the knees of the goddesses and looked earnestly into the eyes of the gods. He even hugged Apollo's knees, saying, "Would I steal from my own dear brother—child of my own beloved father, the mighty, the ineffable Zeus?"

Hera stood up with a scream of rage. "*Another* son of yours, Zeus?"

5 **shyster:** a dishonest person

She pointed a fearsome finger at Hermes. "For that I'll make you sorry you were ever born, baby!" Then she slammed out of the courtroom.

"You were *seen*. There are *witnesses*," snarled Apollo at his little half brother.

Hermes did not even blush, he simply took his tortoise-lyre and began to play. Apollo stared at the extraordinary instrument, overwhelmed with envy.

"I never said I didn't *take* the cows," said Hermes. "I only said I didn't *steal* the cows. The truth is, I merely *borrowed* the cows. For a drink, you know. We babies, we need our milk if we're to grow into big, strong boys. You ladies understand that, surely? Naturally, brother, you can have your cows back whenever you like. And as a token of goodwill, I'd like you to accept this lyre—I invented it yesterday."

The court cheered and clapped. Apollo snatched the lyre and began to pluck at it suspiciously. Zeus got to his feet.

"Hermes, son of Maia, you are plainly a rascal and a rogue. But you have clever fingers and a golden tongue. From this day forward, you shall be messenger of the gods . . . as soon as you have given back Apollo's shining cattle."

"Thank you, Father!" exclaimed Hermes. "Perhaps he might like these back, too." From behind his back, Big Baby Hermes produced the bow and arrow he had stolen from Apollo when he hugged him. The jury of gods gasped and stamped their feet, laughing at the outrageous audacity of the child. Even Apollo could not stay angry with a half brother who had given him the first lyre in the world. They left court together, discussing philosophy and music, poetry and politics.

"You had better watch out for Queen Hera," Apollo warned his little half brother. "She hates you with a deadly hatred. She will never let you be messenger of the gods, no matter what Zeus says."

"Oh, no? Would you like to bet on that?" replied Hermes. "If Hera drives me off Olympus, I shall teach you how to play that lyre of mine. If I make her like me, you can give me . . . what? . . . your magic wand. Agreed?"

"Agreed!" cried Apollo. "You haven't a chance."

"Well, please excuse me now," said Baby Hermes politely, "but it's time for my morning nap." He trotted away across the marble floors of Olympus, toward the hall of the Queen of Heaven.

He went to the cradle at the foot of her bed, and smiled down at her own baby son, Ares.

"Could I ask you a very great favor?" he said.

When Hera returned to her room, she lifted her baby, swaddled in lambswool, and cradled him in her arms. She fed him, she sang to him, she rocked him—"My, what a fine, big boy you are!"—and, plucking back the swaddling from around his head, she kissed his tufty hair.

"Agoo," said Hermes. "Guess who."

It was a risk. She has a nasty temper, the Queen of Heaven. She might have beaten his brains out then and there. But she didn't. They say a woman can't feed a baby and hate it afterward. Hera and Hermes get along well now, so long as he makes himself useful: cooking, running errands. So he won his bet with Apollo—won the magic wand, too, though he still gave Apollo music lessons. In exchange, Apollo taught his half brother how to foretell the future. ∾

Responding to Cluster One

What Are the Qualities of the Gods and Goddesses?

Thinking Skill GENERALIZING

1. Using a chart such as the one below, list the Greek gods and goddesses you learned about from this cluster and **generalize**, or draw a conclusion, about the qualities of each. Choose three words to describe each deity. Look for details and clues in the myths themselves.

Greek God or Goddess	Three Words of Description

2. Choose your favorite myth from this cluster. Explain your choice, telling how it held your interest, what drew you to the characters, and what you liked about the author's style.

3. Imagine you are the casting director of a film called "Olympus: The Movie." Cast the roles of the twelve Olympians with contemporary actors. Use what you have learned in this cluster to help make your decisions.

4. The authors of both "Pandora" and "Big Baby Hermes" use humor as part of their writing styles. One humor technique, **anachronism**, comes from the Greek root *cronos* and means "out of time." For example, a laptop computer would be out of the time period of Greek myths. Find an anachronism in each story.

Writing Activity: Getting to Know Them

Write an introductory essay to a book about gods and goddesses. Use the information you have learned from this cluster to make **generalizations** about the gods and goddesses as you introduce the book.

A Strong Introductory Essay:

- introduces the subject in a general way
- uses interesting examples to capture reader interest
- tells readers what to expect in the book

CLUSTER TWO

How Does Myth Explain Nature?
Thinking Skill COMPARING AND CONTRASTING

FABLE OF ARACHNE
1644–1648
Diego Rodriguez de Silva y Velazquez

Arachne

OLIVIA E. COOLIDGE

Arachne was a maiden who became famous throughout Greece, though she was neither wellborn nor beautiful and came from no great city. She lived in an obscure little village, and her father was a humble dyer of wool. In this he was very skillful, producing many varied shades, while above all he was famous for the clear, bright scarlet which is made from shellfish and which was the most glorious of all the colors used in ancient Greece. Even more skillful than her father was Arachne. It was her task to spin the fleecy wool into a fine, soft thread and to weave it into cloth on the high-standing loom within the cottage. Arachne was small and pale from much working. Her eyes were light and her hair was a dusty brown, yet she was quick and graceful, and her fingers, roughened as they were, went so fast that it was hard to follow their flickering movements. So soft and even was her thread, so fine her cloth, so gorgeous her embroidery, that soon her products were known all over Greece. No one had ever seen the like of them before.

At last Arachne's fame became so great that people used to come from far and wide to watch her working. Even the graceful nymphs would steal in from stream or forest and peep shyly through the dark doorway, watching in wonder the white arms of Arachne as she stood at the loom and threw the shuttle from hand to hand between the hanging threads or drew out the long wool, fine as a hair, from the distaff[1] as she sat spinning. "Surely Athena herself must have taught her," people would murmur to one another. "Who else could know the secret of such marvelous skill?"

Arachne was used to being wondered at, and she was immensely

---

1 **distaff:** a spool or reel used for holding wool

proud of the skill that had brought so many to look on her. Praise was all she lived for, and it displeased her greatly that people should think anyone, even a goddess, could teach her anything. Therefore, when she heard them murmur, she would stop her work and turn round indignantly to say, "With my own ten fingers I gained this skill, and by hard practice from early morning till night. I never had time to stand looking as you people do while another maiden worked. Nor if I had, would I give Athena credit because .the girl was more skillful than I. As for Athena's weaving, how could there be finer cloth or more beautiful embroidery than mine? If Athena herself were to come down and compete with me, she could do no better than I."

One day when Arachne turned round with such words, an old woman answered her, a grey old woman, bent and very poor, who stood leaning on a staff and peering at Arachne amid the crowd of onlookers.

"Reckless girl," she said, "how dare you claim to be equal to the immortal gods themselves? I am an old woman and have seen much. Take my advice and ask pardon of Athena for your words. Rest content with your fame of being the best spinner and weaver that mortal eyes have ever beheld."

"Stupid old woman," said Arachne indignantly, "who gave you a right to speak in this way to me? It is easy to see that you were never good for anything in your day, or you would not come here in poverty and rags to gaze at my skill. If Athena resents my words, let her answer them herself. I have challenged her to a contest, but she, of course, will not come. It is easy for the gods to avoid matching their skill with that of men."

At these words the old woman threw down her staff and stood erect. The wondering onlookers saw her grow tall and fair and stand clad in long robes of dazzling white. They were terribly afraid as they realized that they stood in the presence of Athena. Arachne herself flushed red for a moment, for she had never really believed that the goddess would hear her. Before the group that was gathered there she would not give in; so pressing her pale lips together in obstinacy and pride, she led the goddess to one of the great looms and set herself before the other. Without a word both began to thread the long woolen strands that hung from the rollers and between which the shuttle would move back and forth. Many skeins[2] lay heaped beside them to use, bleached white, and gold, and scarlet, and other shades, varied as the rainbow. Arachne had never thought of giving credit for her success to her father's skill in dyeing, though in actual truth the colors were as remarkable as the cloth itself.

---

2 **skeins:** lengths of loosely coiled thread

Soon there was no sound in the room but the breathing of the onlookers, the whirring of the shuttles, and the creaking of the wooden frames as each pressed the thread up into place or tightened the pegs by which the whole was held straight. The excited crowd in the doorway began to see that the skill of both in truth was very nearly equal but that, however the cloth might turn out, the goddess was the quicker of the two. A pattern of many pictures was growing on her loom. There was a border of twined branches of the olive, Athena's favorite tree, while in the middle, figures began to appear. As they looked at the glowing colors, the spectators realized that Athena was weaving into her pattern a last warning to Arachne. The central figure was the goddess herself, competing with Poseidon for possession of the city of Athens; but in the four corners were mortals who had tried to strive with gods and pictures of the awful fate that had overtaken them. The goddess ended a little before Arachne and stood back from her marvelous work to see what the maiden was doing.

Never before had Arachne been matched against anyone whose skill was equal, or even nearly equal, to her own. As she stole glances from time to time at Athena and saw the goddess working swiftly, calmly, and always a little faster than herself, she became angry instead of frightened, and an evil thought came into her head. Thus, as Athena stepped back a pace to watch Arachne finishing her work, she saw that the maiden had taken for her design a pattern of scenes which showed evil or unworthy actions of the gods, how they had deceived fair maidens, resorted to trickery, and appeared on earth from time to time in the form of poor and humble people. When the goddess saw this insult glowing in bright colors on Arachne's loom, she did not wait while the cloth was judged but stepped forward, her grey eyes blazing with anger, and tore Arachne's work across. Then she struck Arachne across the face. Arachne stood there a moment, struggling with anger, fear, and pride. "I will not live under this insult," she cried, and seizing a rope from the wall, she made a noose and would have hanged herself.

The goddess touched the rope and touched the maiden. "Live on, wicked girl," she said. "Live on and spin, both you and your descendants. When men look at you, they may remember that it is not wise to strive with Athena." At that the body of Arachne shriveled up; and her legs grew tiny, spindly, and distorted. There before the eyes of the spectators hung a little dusty brown spider on a slender thread.

All spiders descend from Arachne, and as the Greeks watched them spinning their thread wonderfully fine, they remembered the contest with Athena and thought that it was not right for even the best of men to claim equality with the gods. ∾

Artemis, Orion and the Seven Sisters

KATHLEEN LINES

Apollo's twin sister often left the councils of Olympus and came to the forests of Arcady. Artemis, who had all wild things in her care and was goddess of the chase, liked to spend long days in the open air hunting, or just wandering through the woods at any time of the year, watching the small animals which lived there. She wore, like any huntress, a simple white tunic[1] and carried javelin[2] and bow and arrows. Her glorious hair was brushed severely back and tied with a single ribbon. Except for her stature and the divine beauty of her face no one would have suspected she was not what she seemed to be. But since the forest was known to be one of the favorite places of the virgin huntress no mortal man dared to penetrate deeply into the woods. When the moon shone the goddess was always present; large and small animals danced before her, and plants too and even the leaves of the trees.

High in the wooded hills was a roomy cave where Artemis could rest and sleep. Here she came, attended by her nymphs, to lay aside bow and quiver and javelin, and change from her hunting tunic into soft garments. They ate wild berries, drank from the mountain spring, and talked and sang and danced. Often on hot summer days Artemis and her companions bathed in the nearby lake. They were happy and free from care, for none, save her maidens, dared follow the goddess to this retreat.

Now one day, while Artemis was deep in the forest pursuing a swift

1 **tunic:** a loosely fitting garment belted at the waist
2 **javelin:** a lightweight spear

stag, great Orion came hunting. He was famous all over Greece. No wild animal, however fierce or cunning, was safe from his club, sword or spear, for he was sure of eye, immensely strong and tall, and very quick on his feet. No mortal man was his equal as a hunter. Orion adored the beautiful goddess of the chase, whose power was greater than his own. Where she went, he followed, but always at a distance. This day, as he skirted the edge of the woods, he saw a glimmer of white in the shadows of the trees and bushes ahead of him. Wanting to discover what animal this could be, he silently made his way forward.

Now it happened that nymphs of the goddess's company had strayed away from the chase, and were resting in the dim shade. They were seven sisters, dressed, like their mistress, in white tunics, and wearing their hair tied with a single ribbon. Suddenly, when they realized that the huge figure of a man was coming stealthily towards them, they sprang to their feet. Orion saw his quarry break out from the shadows into seven white streaks and supposed he had disturbed some rare birds. The nymphs in fright began to run, and Orion followed.

As they crossed a clearing in the woods he saw they were not birds but girls—and, overcome by curiosity, he threw aside his weapons and chased them, and would soon have overtaken them. The terrified nymphs called aloud to Artemis for help. "Immortal goddess, save us!" Artemis heard their cries and, just as Orion's hand was outstretched to catch them, she changed them into birds. Seven white doves flew up and away from the feet of the astonished hunter. Up they flew, and up until they reached the sky. By the command of Zeus they became the cluster of seven stars known as the Seven Sisters, or the Pleiades.

Later Artemis forgave Orion for pursuing her nymphs and allowed him to become her hunting companion. Leaving Arcadia for a time they travelled from forest to forest and plain to plain throughout the world, enjoying great sport. But Apollo did not think it right that his goddess sister should spend so much time with Orion. He chided her, and jeered at her companion—a brawny mortal with no ideas in his simple head beyond adoration of Artemis and the joys of hunting. When his sister paid no heed to him, Apollo became both jealous and angry. He made up his mind to put an end to the friendship. So he watched Artemis and awaited his opportunity. He found her alone one day on the sea shore, watching some little fish.

Apollo knew, although his sister did not, that Orion was swimming far out from land. So, pointing to Orion's head which appeared as a dark object bobbing up and down in the waves, he said, "I shall hit that target with an arrow before you can." Accepting this challenge Artemis quickly fitted an arrow to her bow, and taking aim let fly. She shot true. Her arrow bit deeply into the mark, and she killed Orion. When she realized what she had done she placed his image amongst the stars near the Pleiades, thereby making his name immortal.

Orion rises above the horizon in the autumn, and stands, facing the Pleiades, club in hand ready for Taurus, the Bull, who seems about to charge. From the hunter's jewelled belt hangs his sword, with the great nebulae[3] in its hilt. At his right shoulder gleams the red light of the star Betelgeux, and marking his left foot is the white-hot, brilliant Rigel. Orion's dogs are beside him and all around are animals of the chase. During the cold, crisp months of the year—during the hunting season— Orion, himself the great hunter, is one of the most splendid constellations of the night sky.

The bright cluster of the Pleiades can be seen sparkling in the constellation of Taurus. When Troy was destroyed by the Greeks, Electra, the youngest of the sisters, could not bear to watch the city burn. In a frenzy of grief she left her place in the heavens. Men saw her go, her hair streaming behind her and her garments a blaze of light. The other six stayed and still make a sisterly group. They move through space together, in the same direction and at the same speed; they might be a flock of wild birds. ❧

3 **nebulae:** clouds of gas or dust in space

Demeter and Persephone

PENELOPE PRODDOW, TRANSLATOR

Now I will sing
of golden-haired Demeter,
the awe-inspiring goddess,
and of her trim-ankled daughter,
Persephone,
who was frolicking in a grassy meadow.

She was far away
from her mother.

With the deep-girdled daughters of Ocean,
the maiden was gathering flowers—
crocuses, roses and violets,
irises and lovely hyacinths
growing profusely together,
with one narcissus . . .[1]

This was the snare
for the innocent maiden.

She knelt in delight
to pluck the astonishing bloom
when, all of a sudden, the wide-wayed earth
split open
down the Nysian[2] meadow.

Out sprang a lord
with his deathless horses.
It was He Who Receives Many Guests,
He Who Has Many Names.

1 **narcissus:** family of flowers with white or yellow blossoms such as daffodils
   or jonquils
2 **Nysian:** in the region of the Nysa mountain in ancient Greece

THE RETURN OF PERSEPHONE
1891
Frederic Leighton

Seizing Persephone,
he caught her up in his golden chariot
despite her laments.

Her screams were shrill
as she shrieked for her father, Zeus,
but no one heard
except kind-hearted Hecate
from her cave
and Helios, the sun.

Still glimpsing the earth,
the brilliant sky,
the billowing, fish-filled sea
and the rays of the sun,
Persephone vainly hoped to see her beloved mother again.

The peaks of the mountains
and the ocean depths
resounded
with her immortal voice.

And her stately mother heard.
A sudden pang
went through Demeter's heart.

She set off like a bird
wildly
over the bodies of water
and the dry stretches of land,
but no one would tell her the truth—
not a god,
not a mortal,
not even a long-winged bird of omen.

She circled the earth
for nine days
steadily,
brandishing shining torches.

At the dawning
of the tenth,
Hecate approached,
holding a pine torch in her hands.

"Demeter!" she said.
"Bringer of the Seasons!
Giver of Rich Gifts!
What god in heaven,
what mortal,
has caused your heart such torment
and taken your daughter?
I heard her cries
but I did not see
who he was!"

They both hurried on
to the sun,
the watchman of gods and of men.

"Helios!" cried Demeter.
"Have pity on me—goddess that I am.
I bore a child
whose frantic voice I heard
through the barren air
as if she had been overpowered,
but I saw nothing.
Tell me,
was it a god or a mortal
who stole away my daughter
against her will—and mine?"

"Fair-tressed Demeter!" Helios replied.
"No one is guilty
among the immortals
but Zeus,
who gave her to Hades
to be his youthful bride.

"Now, Goddess,
you must stop this violent weeping!

"The Ruler of Many is not undesirable
as a son-in-law.
He wields great power,
for he is king over the dead,
with whom he lives
in the underworld."

Anguish
rent the goddess' heart—
savage and terrible.

Embittered with black-clouded Zeus,
she departed broad Olympus
and the gatherings of the gods.
From that time forth,
she sought the villages and fields of mortal men
with her face disguised.

. . . Golden-haired Demeter
remained
enthroned within [her temple],
far from all of the festive gods,
wasting away with longing
for her graceful daughter.

She made that year
most shocking and frightening
for mortals
who lived on the nourishing earth.

The soil did not yield a single seed—
Demeter kept them all
underground.

In vain,
oxen hauled many curved ploughs
over the meadows.

Now, she was about to cause
the race of chattering men

to die out
altogether
from frightful hunger,
depriving those who lived on Olympus
of their lavish gifts and sacrifices.

Then Zeus noticed . . .

He sent golden-winged Iris first
to summon her.
On swift feet,
Iris spanned the distance
to Eleusis[3]—now laden with incense—
and found Demeter
within her temple,
clad in a dark gown.

"Demeter!" she announced.
"Father Zeus
in his infinite wisdom
calls you back to the family
of the undying gods."

Demeter's heart was unmoved.

Thereupon Zeus
sent forth all the gods—
the joyous beings who live forever.

Demeter scorned their speeches.
She vowed
she would not set foot on Olympus
nor let a fruit spring up on the earth
until she had seen
with her own eyes
the lovely face of her daughter.

Then Zeus dispatched Hermes
with his staff of gold.

3 **Eleusis:** Greek site of Demeter's temple

Setting off from the Olympian seat,
Hermes dashed down
at once
into the depths of the earth.

He found Hades
in his halls
on a couch with his tender bride—
who was listless
out of longing for her mother.

"Dark-haired Hades!" said Hermes
"Zeus commands me
to bring back fair Persephone.
Her mother is planning a horrible deed—
to starve the tribes
of earth-dwelling mortals
and so, to deprive the gods
of their offerings!"

The king of the dead
raised his eyebrows,
but he did not disobey Zeus' order.

"Go, Persephone," he said,
"back to your dark-robed mother!"
Persephone smiled,
as joyfully she sprang up from the couch,
but stealthily the lord of the dead
spread out about her
delicious pomegranate[4] seeds
to make sure she would not remain
forever
at the side of her noble mother.

Soon after, Hades
harnessed up his deathless horses
to the golden chariot.

---

4 **pomegranate:** a thick-skinned fruit with reddish pulp and many seeds

Persephone leapt into the car.
Hermes seized the whip and the reins
in his skillful hands
and they drove off together
away from the land of the dead.

Hermes guided the horses
to Eleusis where Demeter sat
waiting,
and they drew to a halt
in front of her incense-filled temple.
Demeter,
catching sight of Persephone,
flew forward
like a maenad[5] on a mountain.

But, as she clasped her daughter,
she suspected treachery.

"My child!" she cried in fear.
"Could you have eaten anything
in the land of the dead?"

"Truthfully, Mother!"
exclaimed Persephone.
"When Hermes arrived from Zeus,
I arose with joy.
Then Hades brought out delicious pomegranate seeds
and urged me to eat them."

"In that case,
you must return
to the land of the dead," said Demeter,
"for one third of the rolling seasons.

"But when you come back
to me
for the other two,

---

5 **maenad:** an exciteable female participant in a ritual honoring Dionysus, the
   god of wine and revelry

the earth will burst into bloom
with flocks of sweet-smelling, spring flowers—
a great marvel to all men."

At that moment,
Wide-ruling Zeus
sent a messenger—
Rhea
with a golden band in her hair.

"Demeter, my daughter," said Rhea,
"Zeus wishes you
to return to the company of the gods.
Yield to him,
lest you carry your anger
toward dark-clouded Zeus
too far.

"And now,
bestow some nourishing fruit
on mortal men!"

Bright-garlanded Demeter
did not disobey.

Immediately, she caused the fruit
to grow in the fertile fields
and soon the wide earth
was weighed down
with buds and blossoms.

Hail to you, Demeter,
Lady of fragrant Eleusis,
Leader of the Seasons and Giver of Shining Gifts,
you and your most beautiful daughter Persephone,
look kindly on me
and in return for my song,
grant abundant life to follow.

Persephone, Falling

RITA DOVE

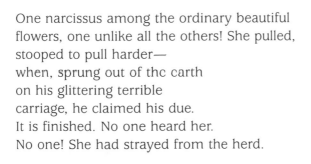

One narcissus among the ordinary beautiful
flowers, one unlike all the others! She pulled,
stooped to pull harder—
when, sprung out of the earth
on his glittering terrible
carriage, he claimed his due.
It is finished. No one heard her.
No one! She had strayed from the herd.

(Remember: go straight to school.
This is important, stop fooling around!
Don't answer to strangers. Stick
with your playmates. Keep your eyes down.)
This is how easily the pit
opens. This is how one foot sinks into the ground.

Echo and Narcissus

ANNE TERRY WHITE

Of all the mountain nymphs, none was more charming than Echo. But she had one fault. She talked too much. It was chatter, chatter all day long, and no matter what the subject, Echo always had the last word.

Now one day when Zeus was enjoying the company of the nymphs, Hera suddenly appeared. All hurried to get away except Echo, who, to distract the goddess, started to talk. She kept Hera amused so long that the nymphs made their escape. But Hera was furious when she found out how she had been deceived.

"You shall never get the chance to do it again," she told Echo. "That amusing tongue of yours shall lose its power. From now on it will never be able to start chattering, nor do anything except the one thing you are so fond of—reply. Yes, indeed, you shall have the last word, Echo. But that is all you will have! Never will you be able to speak *first*!"

Soon after this, Echo found out just how bad her punishment was. She fell in love, and, as luck would have it, with a young hunter who could not love anybody but himself. Narcissus was an exceptionally handsome youth. But he was as cold as he was handsome.

Poor Echo trailed all over the mountains after Narcissus. How she longed to speak to him and win his love by gentle words! Alas, she had not the power!

Then one day while Narcissus was hunting, it happened that he became separated from his companions.

"Who's here?" he shouted.

"Here!" Echo replied.

Narcissus looked around. He could see no one.

"Come!" he called.

Echo immediately answered, "Come!"

Narcissus waited, but when no one came, he called again: "Why do you keep away from me?"

"Away from me!" Echo called back.

"Let us meet!" Narcissus said.

"Let us meet!" the nymph agreed with all her heart. She ran to the spot, arms upraised and ready to throw around his neck.

Narcissus started back. "Do not touch me!" he cried. "I would rather die than that you should have me!"

"Have me!" Echo pleaded.

But in vain. The young man strode off, leaving the nymph to hide her blushes in the thick woods.

From that time on, Echo would never show herself. Caves and mountain cliffs became her home. Her body wasted away with grief and longing until all her flesh was gone. Her bones changed into rocks. And nothing was left of her but her voice, with which she still replies to anyone who calls.

Cruel Narcissus! Echo was not the only being whose heart he broke. But at last he got what he deserved. A maiden whom he had spurned asked the goddess of vengeance to take her part.

"Oh, may the time come," the girl prayed, "when Narcissus may feel what it is to love and get no love in return!"

And the avenging goddess heard. . . .

▲　▲　▲

There was a sparkling spring in the hills, to which for some reason shepherds never drove their flocks. Neither did mountain goats nor any beasts of the forest ever drink from it. Fresh green grass grew all around, and rocks sheltered the spring from the sun. The water in the pool was as clear as polished silver. Not a dead branch, not a dead leaf polluted it.

To this pool one day Narcissus came, worn out with hunting, hot and thirsty. He stooped down to drink—and saw his lovely image in the water.

"It is the water-spirit," he thought, for he had never seen his own reflection before. Enchanted, he knelt down to look and could not take his gaze away. He bent close to place a kiss upon the parted lips, and stretched out his arms to clasp the lovely being. At his touch the image dissolved into a thousand ripples. But even as he watched, it came back as clear as before.

"Beautiful being," Narcissus said, "why do you flee from me? Surely my face cannot displease you, for every nymph of the mountains is in love with me, and you yourself look as if you are not indifferent. Your smile answers mine. When I stretch out my arms to you, you do the same."

Tears of longing rolled down his cheeks and splashed into the silver pool. At once the image fled again.

"Stay, oh, stay!" he pleaded. "If I may not touch you, let me at least gaze upon you!"

He was unable to tear himself away. Day after day he hung over the water, feasting his eyes on his own reflection. Love, which he had so often scorned, now so consumed him that he lost his color and was no more than a waxy image of himself. All he could do was sigh, "Alas! Alas!" And Echo answered him, "Alas!"

At last Narcissus faded away altogether and passed from the upper world. But even as his shade[1] was being ferried to the regions of the dead, it looked down into the river Styx to catch a last beloved reflection. The nymphs who had given their hearts to him heaped wood into a funeral pile and would have burned his body, as the custom was. But his remains were nowhere to be found. Only a wax-white flower with a purple heart stood in the place where he had knelt and sighed. And to this flower the grieving maidens gave his name—Narcissus. ∾

---

1 **shade:** spirit; ghost

Narcissus at 60

LINDA PASTAN

If love hadn't made him clumsy,
if he hadn't fallen forward,
had never drowned
in his own perfection,

what would he have thought
about his aging face
as it altered, year after year
season by season?

In the old conspiracy
between the eye
and its reflection, love casts
a primal shadow.

Perhaps he would blame
the wrinkling surface of the pool
for what he saw
or think the blemishes

on his once smooth cheek
were simply small fish
just beneath the lethal skin
of the water.

METAMORPHOSIS OF NARCISSUS   1937   Salvador Dali

Responding to Cluster Two

How Does Myth Explain Nature?

Thinking Skill COMPARING AND CONTRASTING

1. To better understand how the ancients used myth to explain nature, use a chart such as the one below to choose several natural events described in this cluster. **Compare and contrast** scientific and mythical explanations for them.

Scientific Explanations	Natural Events	Classical Myth Explanations
occurs during a weather change when atmosphere discharges electricity	*lightning*	*Zeus is angry and throws a thunderbolt*

2. "Arachne" has a clear **moral**, best summed up in Athena's final statement to Arachne: ". . . it is not wise to strive with [gods/goddesses]." Look at the selections about Persephone and Narcissus and write a moral that best states the themes of these two tales.

3. A **Homeric epithet** is a description such as "swift-footed Achilles" or "sweet-smelling flowers." A stylistic element often used in classical Greek literature, it generally uses two adjectives linked by a hyphen. List three examples of Homeric epithets in "Demeter and Persephone." Then pick two other characters from this cluster and use a Homeric epithet to describe them either seriously or humorously.

4. **Compare and contrast** the two goddesses, Artemis and Athena. How are they similar and how are they different?

5. Name and chart constellations for Arachne, Persephone, and Narcissus.

Writing Activity: Myth in the Making

Choose one of the following natural events and create your own mythological explanation of its origin: volcano, meteorite, flood, ozone hole, smog, lunar/solar eclipse, black hole, or erosion.

A Myth That Explains Nature

- employs imagination to explain natural events
- uses vivid language
- holds the reader's interest
- uses the elements of a good story, such as plot and character development

CLUSTER THREE

How Does Myth Explain Human Nature?
Thinking Skill   EVALUATING

Homer, the Blind Poet

ALISOUN WITTING

READING FROM HOMER   1885   Sir Lawrence Alma-Tadema

The meal was finished. The Greek warriors and lords leaned back on their couches and took up deep cups of wine mixed with honey, as the great hall grew darker before the oncoming night. Torches, oil-lamps, and the flames from a huge fireplace illuminated the smoky interior of the hall with leaping tongues of light and shadow. All members of the household—servants, women, and those children who had begged to stay up or managed to slip out of bed—began to assemble quietly about the fireplace, for tonight was a very special night: among the guests at table was a bard,

a singer of tales, who would entertain the company with hours of song in return for their hospitality. Presently the lord at the head of the table spoke courteously to his guest: "Friend, if you are now well rested and have eaten your fill, will you honor us with a song?"

The bard stood up. He was a strong-looking, middle-aged man, attended by a boy who handed him his harp and led him to a seat—for the poet was blind. He sat awhile and tightened the strings of his instrument, thinking of the tale he would sing and the words he would use to sing it. Then, striking his harp, he began a story of war waged for the sake of a beautiful woman and of the battles of heroic men on either side: of the noble prince Hector who fought to defend his walled city Troy from the Greek invaders, and of the Greek lord Menelaus, whose lovely wife Helen was stolen from his home by a Trojan boy. In particular he sang of the Greek hero Achilles, of his nobility and his anger, his quarrel with the Greek commander Agamemnon, the brother of Menelaus, and the consequences of this quarrel.

He chanted his story for a long while, so long that everyone forgot the time and the fire died down to glowing logs before he had finished for the night. The story he sang was well-known to everyone, but the way in which the bard told it brought life and color and passion to the old legends. The battles of Greek and Trojan, and the flaming towers of Troy, were as vivid and real to these Greeks as the battles they themselves had fought.

Who was this Greek poet? Legend says that his name was Homer, that he was blind, and that he composed the two earliest works of Western literature, the *Iliad*, about the Trojan war, and the *Odyssey*, concerning the wanderings of the Greek general Odysseus after the fall of Troy. We do not know whether Homer really existed. The important thing is that there were poets like Homer who sang for their living and wandered from city to city, receiving welcome, hospitality, and a crowd of eager listeners wherever they went.

These poets did not write down their songs, although writing had been invented, the alphabet used was about three times as large as the later Greek alphabet, and writing was a very slow, awkward process, good for bookkeeping but hopelessly unsuited to heroic poetry. Nor did the bard memorize the lines of his poems—he would compose and sing in the same breath, never breaking the meter[1] of his poem, never losing the action of his story. It is a manner of story-telling that has almost disappeared from the modern world, for books, radio, television, movies, and the automobile offer so much entertainment to us now that story-telling has ceased to be the art that it was.

But to the Mycenean Greeks of the 8th century B.C., it was storytellers such as Homer who brought beauty, interest, and the Greek ideals of courage and excellence into their everyday lives. ∾

---

1 **meter:** rhythm

Odysseus

W.H.D. Rouse

At last the Trojan war was over; it is a long story, well worth your hearing, but I cannot tell it all now. I must tell you, however, of the adventures of one of the men who went home.

This was Odysseus of Ithaca. Now Ithaca is a small and rocky island, which lies in the sea west of Greece, not far south of Corfu. All the islands in this group once belonged to England, only [they] gave them back to the King of Greece after the Greeks made themselves free of the Turks. It is a lovely island, full of flowers, and the people are kind, and still very proud of their great man, Odysseus, after three thousand years.

Odysseus had left behind him his wife, named Penelope, whom he loved so much that all he wanted was to go home again and be at peace. When he bade good-bye to her, and his baby son Telemachos, he said, "My wife, I may be killed in the war. If I die, bring up our son to be a good man, and when he is old enough to manage the house, I hope you will marry again and be happy." But she said, "My husband, I want no one but you." He was away for twenty years: the siege lasted for ten years, and he took ten years to get home, but when he arrived, he found her waiting for him. And this is the story.

Odysseus set sail from Troy with his countrymen of Ithaca and the islands round about, twelve ships in all. They were blown far away to the west of the Mediterranean Sea, and when the wind fell, they came to land in a lovely country. The people welcomed those who went on shore, and gave them to eat of the fruit of the country, the lotus, which they lived on, sweet as honey. Anyone who ate of it wished never to come away, but only to go on forever eating the sweet lotus. It seemed to be always afternoon, and nobody wanted to do any more work for ever and ever. But Odysseus would not have that. He carried off the lazy men, and tied them down under the benches, until the ships were well away.

By and by the wind took them to a little wild island, and Odysseus went off with one ship to explore. As he came near the mainland, he saw an enclosure upon the hillside, full of sheep and goats; so he took a few men with him, and climbed up to the place. They found a great cave within the walls of the enclosure. There were pens for lambs, and pens for kids: rows and rows of cheeses, pans and jars full of whey[1] or milk. They helped themselves to milk and cheese, and roasted a lamb, and enjoyed themselves.

By and by a horrible monster approached, big and hairy, and they ran and hid in the cave. He milked all the sheep and goats, and curdled the milk: then he lit a fire, and saw the men.

"Who are you, stranger?" he asked.

Odysseus said, "Sir, we are strangers from Troy; have pity on us, for Zeus is the god of strangers."

"Pooh, pooh!" he said—"Zeus! We care nothing for Zeus, or any gods: we are stronger than they are."

He stretched out his hands, and caught two of the men, and dashed them like puppies on the ground, so that their brains ran out. Then he carved them limb from limb, and ate them for his supper, and slept.

This monster was a Cyclops, named Polyphemos. You remember that dreadful brood of creatures, and the three who were guardians of fire in the early days.

Next morning, the Cyclops killed and ate two more men, and went about his work. But he rolled a huge stone in front of the cave, so that no one could get out.

But Odysseus was never at a loss for a plan. He picked up a sapling of olive wood which lay in the cave, and smoothed it, and made it ready; and he chose out four good men to help him, when the night should come.

In the evening, the Cyclops drove in all his rams, and rolled the great stone in front of the door; next, as before, he killed and ate two more men for supper. Then Odysseus came up to him, bearing a skin of wine which he had brought from the ship, and he said, "Cyclops, here, have a drink after your supper!"

He drank it, and it pleased him so much that he said, "Another,

---

1 **whey:** watery part of milk, most often used to make cheese

please!" Odysseus gave him another, and another still, and he said, "Indeed, this is fine stuff, better than our wine! I must give you a stranger's gift for this. What is your name?"

"My name," said Odysseus, "is Noman."

"Very well, Noman, your gift shall be, that I will eat you last of all."

Then he lay down, and went to sleep, grunting and growling.

There was Odysseus, and there were his men, shut up in the cave, and they could not get out; for the stone was too heavy for them to move. But Odysseus had his plan ready.

He took the olive-sapling, and buried it under the ashes; and when it was red hot, he made his four men hold it straight, while he pushed the point hard into the eye of the Cyclops; for he has only one eye, as you remember, in the middle of his forehead, with a thick bushy eyebrow running right across his face. The red-hot point burnt the eyeball, which sizzled like fat in the fire.

The Cyclops roared aloud, and pulled out the stake, and threw it from him, and the men ran off and hid in the corners of the cave. The Cyclops made such a noise, that all the other Cyclopes came running up to the cave, and called out, "Why are you making all that noise? Is anyone killing you?" Polyphemos replied, "Noman is killing me!" Then they said,

ULYSSES BLINDING POLYPHEMUS   Pellegrino Tibaldi

"If no man is killing you, you must just pray to God; what is the use of waking us all out of our sleep?" And they went away, but Odysseus laughed to himself at the success of his trick.

Then he caught up the long withies[2] that lay on the floor in a heap, and tied his men each under one of the fleecy rams, with another ram tied to this ram on each side. He picked the biggest ram of all for himself, and waited for morning.

In the morning, the Cyclops rolled back the stone from the door of the cave, and let his rams out, holding out his hands, and feeling their backs; but he did not feel underneath, so the men all got safely out, fastened together in threes. Odysseus came last, hanging on underneath the biggest ram of all. And so they escaped from the Cyclops. But this Cyclops was a son of Poseidon, and ever afterwards Poseidon hated Odysseus and did his best to destroy him.

They all sailed away, until they reached the island of Aiolos, the steward of the winds. Aiolos wished to help Odysseus on his way; so he bottled up all the winds in a leather bag, except the West Wind, which was to blow them home. They went bowling along for nine days, until they actually came in sight of Ithaca, their home; and then Odysseus, tired out, fell asleep.

While he was asleep, the sailors eyed this bag, and one said to another, "I wonder what Aiolos gave him. Gold and silver, to be sure! let us see." So they opened the mouth of the bag, and all the winds poured out, and began to blow together, north, south, east, and west, and blew them far away. They had many adventures, which I cannot tell of now, but after a long time they came to land in a pleasant island, and Odysseus sent some of his men to explore.

They found a fine house among the trees; and as they came near, what should they see but all sorts of animals, lions and tigers, leopards and wild boars, which did them no harm; they just ran up, wagging their tails, and barking in a friendly way. The men all went in, except one, who remained to watch.

Within the hall was a woman, singing sweetly as she plied the loom. She gave them welcome, and provided a good feast; and when they had eaten, she tapped each with her stick, and said, "Away to the sty with you!" At once their hair changed into bristles, and they turned into pigs, and ran away into the sty.

2 **withies:** twigs or branches

The watcher reported to Odysseus that the others had all disappeared; and Odysseus himself went to explore. On the way, he met the god Hermes, who gave him a magic root which would protect him against enchantments. So when he came to the house of Circe—that was the witch's name—she had no power over him, and he compelled her to change his men back to their proper shape.

Circe was a good friend to them after this, and helped them with advice, and gave them all they wanted. Odysseus had to visit the dark Kingdom of Hades, where he received directions for his homeward voyage. And on the way back he had many other dangers to face.

He had to pass by the island of the Sirens. These were witches who looked like birds; they sang so sweetly, that everyone who heard them felt obliged to land. There they sat in a meadow, singing, and all round them were the shrivelled bodies of the men who had come to hear, and sat down and listened, until they died. Odysseus was warned of this by Circe; and before he came to the island, he plugged up all the ears of all his men with wax, so that they should not hear. But he wanted to hear himself, yet not to be hurt; so he told his men to tie him to the mast, and not to let him loose, whatever happened.

Then they rowed on. Soon the lovely song of the Sirens was heard, and Odysseus struggled to get free, and shouted to his men to let him loose; but they rowed on, until they were safe out of hearing.

Next they had to pass between Scylla and Charybdis. On one side of a strait was Charybdis, where a whirlpool three times a day sucked up the water, and spouted it out again: no ship could live in that whirlpool. On the other side was a rock, and on this rock in a cave lived a monster, Scylla, with twelve legs, and six long necks with heads like dogs; and if a ship passed by, she curled down her six necks, and caught up a sailor with each head. This is what she did to Odysseus and his crew.

After this, all his ships were destroyed in a frightful storm, but Odysseus himself was saved, and washed up on another island. On this island lived another witch, Calypso, who saved him, and kept him there for seven long years. She wanted him for a husband, and she offered to make him immortal; but he refused, because all he wanted was to return to his beloved wife Penelope. And he did return, and did find his wife waiting for him, although he had to fight a terrible battle with his enemies before he won her again. But after all his troubles, he spent with his wife a peaceful and quiet old age. ❧

Siren Song

MARGARET ATWOOD

This is the one song everyone
would like to learn: the song
that is irresistable:

the song that forces men
to leap overboard in squadrons
even though they see the beached skulls

the song nobody knows
because anyone who has heard it
is dead, and the others can't remember.

Shall I tell you the secret
and if I do, will you get me
out of this bird suit?

I don't enjoy it here
squatting on this island
looking picturesque and mythical

with these two feathery maniacs,
I don't enjoy singing
this trio, fatal and valuable.

I will tell the secret to you,
to you, only to you.
Come closer. This song

is a cry for help. Help me!
Only you, only you can,
you are unique

at last. Alas
it is a boring song
but it works every time.

ODYSSEUS AND THE SIRENS
1919
Edmund Dulac

Cupid and Psyche

BARBARA MCBRIDE-SMITH

Cupid was a mama's boy. It wasn't his fault. She wouldn't let go of him. She practically hogtied him with her apron strings. You know how mamas are about their babies. So what if Cupid was already thirty-something! He would always be her own little cherub.

Cupid had a hard time shaking that image. Let's face it, Cupid has been the official poster child for Valentine's Day for several thousand years. Cute little naked baby, chubby cheeks, curly locks. Teeny-tiny wings, itsy-bitsy bow with miniature arrows. Goes around shooting people with his arrows, and they fall in love and live happily ever after. Sound about right?

Well, forget about it!

Cupid grew up a long time ago. Grew up tall, blond, and handsome. Still had those wings and still shot people with those love arrows. In fact, he was the god of love, but his mama's apron strings were tying him down.

Cupid's mama was Aphrodite, and she had problems of her own. Years ago she had won a golden apple in a beauty contest, and she figured that settled the beauty question once and for all. So if she heard of another woman who was supposed to be really beautiful, she'd pitch a fit. Then she'd send her son Cupid out to ruin that woman's life with his bow and arrows.

Let me tell you about the power of those arrows. If you got shot with one, you'd turn into a seething mass of desire, a hunka-hunka burnin' love. Then you'd start to put the moves on the very next creature you laid eyes on. Let's say you were out having a business lunch with your boss, and you got hit by one of Cupid's arrows. Because of the scene you'd make right there on the spot, you could lose your job—or get a great big pay raise. Either way, they sure wouldn't let you back in the Burger King anymore. You see what I mean about those arrows?

Well, there was a mortal girl named Psyche who was absolutely gorgeous. She had two older sisters. Remember the two sisters in "Cinderella"? How about the two sisters in "Beauty and the Beast"? OK, Psyche's sisters—same song, second verse. Anyway, Psyche was so beautiful people began to call her the "new and improved Aphrodite." That really got on Aphrodite's nerves a right smart. When her jealousy hit the overflow mark, she called to her son: "Cupid!"

"Yes, Mama?"

"Cupid, I need you to teach that little trollop[1] named Psyche a lesson."

"Sure thing, Mama."

"I want you to shoot her with one of your arrows. And I want the next thing she sees to be the ugliest creature in the universe. She'll fall in love with it and live a life of shame, degradation, and misery."

"All right, Mama. How about a giant two-headed spider?"

"Not bad enough."

"How abut a Cyclops?"

"Not nearly bad enough."

"A Minotaur, Mama?"

"Son, lots of women are married to guys that are half-bull, half-man! What I want is a Texas redneck. I want one with tobacco juice running out the corners of his mouth, a beer can in his hand, and his belly hanging over his belt. I want a muddy pickup truck with a gun rack in the back window and a big ol' hound dog in the front seat. Am I making myself clear, Son?"

"Yes, ma'am. I've never seen you this mad before, but you got it!"

Cupid found Psyche taking a nap beside a stream. He hid behind a bush, got his bow and arrow lined up, and waited for the first pickup truck to come along. Then Psyche rolled over and Cupid got a good look at her face. "Wow!" he said, jumping back. "This is one beautiful girl." As he jumped back, he stabbed himself in the leg with his very own arrow.

That was Cupid's first experience with the idea that what goes around comes around. He fell crazy in love with Psyche, but he couldn't do a

---

1 **trollop:** vulgar woman

thing about it because his mama might be watching. So Cupid hot-winged it outta there and hid for a while, trying to figure out how he could marry Psyche and still keep his mama happy—'cause if Mama ain't happy, ain't nobody happy. Meanwhile he laid some magic on Psyche so she would stay unmarried while he worked out a plan. He wasn't taking any chances on losing her.

Time passed and both of Psyche's older sisters got married to kings. Psyche was still as lovely as ever, but no suitors came to call. Psyche's parents got so worried, they went to an oracle—you know, a for-tuneteller—and asked for advice. The oracle told them the sad and mysterious news: Psyche was destined to marry a non-human winged creature with a poisonous bite. The fortune included instructions to buy her a black wedding dress and leave her on a mountaintop where her husband could find her.

When the parents broke the news to Psyche, she began to weep qui-etly. Her two older sisters carried on like they really cared. "Oh, Psyche! What a shame. You have to marry a monster. Maybe it's a dragon. Maybe it's a great big snake. Married to a snake. Imagine that! What a shame, especially with you being so beautiful and all. We're really sorry. Well, goodbye and good luck. Maybe we'll see you later. Maybe not!"

Psyche put on her black bridal gown and was delivered to the designated mountaintop to wait for her husband. Suddenly a great wind swept her off the mountain and carried her to the place where her husband lived. It turned out to be the most luxurious place Psyche had ever seen. The facilities included exquisitely maintained gardens, crystal-clear fountains, and a magnificent palace inlaid with gold and silver and ivory. Within the palace was a twenty-four-hour gourmet kitchen. Invisible servants met Psyche's every need. And each night, in utter darkness, her husband came to Psyche's room, held her close, and told her how much he adored her. As kind as he was, he never allowed Psyche to see him. She promised she wouldn't try. Each morning, Psyche woke up smiling. Life just doesn't get any better than this, she thought.

Months went by, and one day Psyche received a note from her sisters. They wanted to drop by for a visit, someday when her husband wasn't home. They weren't fond of snakes, they said. That night in the darkness when she told her husband, he said to her, "Not a good idea. Those sis-ters of yours are just trouble waiting for a place to happen."

"Perhaps they've changed. Besides, they're family. You know what they say, 'You can pick your friends . . .' Oh, never mind. Anyway, I miss them . . . sort of. It's just a short visit. What bad could happen?"

"OK, but I hope you know what you're doing," said the monster-husband. "A word to the wise: If they try to talk you into taking a peek at me, don't do it. Otherwise, it's all over for us. I'm a very private person. I'm in a . . . a witness protection program. You can love me without looking at me, can't you? Trust me on this."

The next day the wind shuttle was arranged and the two sisters showed up for their visit. They looked around at the facilities and said, "What's going on here? This place is ten times nicer than ours, and we're married to kings! Are you gonna try to make us believe you get all this from a snake? Never heard of a snake this rich. You sure he's a snake and not just some big west Texas billionaire trying to hide from the government? What's that you say? You've never even laid eyes on him because he only shows up here when it's dark? Oooo, baby sister, you *do* have a problem. Everything that goes around in the dark ain't Santa Claus. No telling what kind of a creep he is. You better get a look at this monster and terminate him before he does it to you first."

By the time the sisters left, Psyche was terribly upset and confused. She said to herself, "Maybe I need to shed a little light on this situation and snitch a peek at him. I know I promised I wouldn't, but what's he trying to hide?"

That night, Psyche took an oil lamp and a knife to bed with her. After her husband arrived and fell asleep, she got out of bed, lit the lamp, held the knife ready, and leaned over the sleeping form. "Wow!" she said, jumping back. "This is one good-looking monster! Wait a minute, this is . . . it's . . . no, it can't be. Cupid, the god of love? And he's mine?"

Now it so happened that while she was jumping back, Psyche sloshed the oil in that lamp. A drop of it ran down the side of the lamp and fell on Cupid's shoulder and burned him, ever so slightly. His eyes opened, and when he saw Psyche looking at him, he said, *"Sweetest things turn sourest by their deeds. Lilies that fester smell far worse than weeds."* Which meant: "You didn't trust me, so I can't trust you, and now I gotta go."

Cupid flew out the window, and so did Psyche's happiness. She was miserable. Her curiosity and suspicions had ruined her idyllic life. The next morning, she set out searching for Cupid. She searched for days but found no trace of him. Finally, in desperation, she went to his mama for help.

Meanwhile, guess who was giving aid and comfort to her baby boy? Mama! And she began to suspect that his melancholy mood was more than homesickness. Eventually it dawned on Aphrodite that Cupid was pining for Psyche. She suggested that he take a vacation at one of her resorts and try to forget whatever garbage was cluttering his head.

The next morning when Aphrodite looked out her window and saw Psyche coming, she got mad enough to eat nails. By now she had learned all the details of Cupid's scheme to keep his marriage to this mortal a secret. Aphrodite said to herself, "I'll work this girl half to death and I won't feed her much. She'll get skinny and ugly and Cupid will forget all about her. Oh yes! The golden apple and my son are still mine!"

But what Aphrodite said to Psyche was this: "Sure, hon, I'll be glad to help you find Cupid. Tell you what, you do a few little tasks for me, and I'll put the word out to all my contacts. My sweet boy will be so happy that you came to see me."

Aphrodite took Psyche into a room where a huge box sat in the middle of the floor. "Look at this, hon. Somebody mixed up my grain shipment from Demeter. If you can get it all sorted into appropriate piles for me by morning, I'll see what I can do about finding Cupid." Aphrodite walked out and locked the door.

Psyche looked in that box, and it was full of cereal. There were corn flakes and bran flakes and wheat flakes. There were Sugar Pops and Cheerios and Count Choculas. There were Rice Chex and Grape-Nuts and bite-size, frosted Shredded Wheats. And they were in total disarray. Psyche took out a handful and began making piles. It seemed to take forever. She could never finish the whole box by morning. Just then, an army of ants crawled under the door. One tiny ant with sergeant stripes on its front legs stepped forward and saluted. "At your service, ma'am. Please step aside. All right, soldiers, let's move it!" Those ants formed themselves into twenty columns, scaled the side of that box, and began sorting the cereals. In short order, the job was done. Hmm, now who do you suppose was behind this helpful little trick?

Aphrodite walked back into the room the next morning and got so mad she wanted to slap Psyche into next week. But she didn't. Instead she gave Psyche two more impossible tasks to do, involving a herd of terrorist sheep who happened to have golden fleece and a goblet of mineral water located atop an ice-covered mountain. With the help of various species of talking plants and animals, sent by a certain secret pal, Psyche was able to pull off both jobs in record time.

Now Aphrodite was really [ticked off]! But she just smiled through her clenched teeth and said, "Psyche, go to Hades! . . . and get me a box of beauty."

"I beg your pardon?" Psyche was certain she had misunderstood.

"Beauty. A box of it. Hades' wife, Persephone Korene, gets it for me wholesale. I'm feeling a little frayed around the edges, need to restore myself, so hurry and get back here with it. And whatever you do, *don't* open up that box and borrow any of my beauty. Maybe I'd better say that again, dear. *Don't* open up that box."

Psyche set off, looking for the road to Hades' underground kingdom. She passed a talking tower. What luck! The tower told her to take two quarters and three dog biscuits with her. "Never mind why, just do it!" said the tower as it pointed her in the right direction. She came to a river called the Styx. A ferryboat driver named Charon offered her a ride. Halfway across, he stopped the boat and held out his hand. Psyche placed a dog biscuit in his palm. Charon snarled, "Cut the funny stuff, lady."

"Oops! Sorry," said Psyche, switching the biscuit for a quarter. Charon then took her to the other side of the river, where she was greeted by Cerberus, a three-headed dog.

"Let me guess. Biscuits!" she tossed the doggie treats to the three heads and dashed through the gates to Hades' kingdom. She got the box from Persephone Korene and hurried out past the dog while the mouths were still chewing. She crossed the river, using her last quarter, and started up the road to Aphrodite's house. Along the way, Psyche said to herself, "I'm feeling a little frayed around the edges myself. I look like something the cat dragged in and the dog wouldn't eat. Cupid will never recognize me like this. I could use a little beauty right now. I wonder why I'm not supposed to open up this box?"

(Yo, Psyche! Does the name Pandora ring a bell?)

Psyche went right ahead and opened up the box . . . and there wasn't any beauty in it at all! That box was full of eternal sleep. The sleep jumped out, grabbed Psyche, and she dropped like a rock.

Now who do you suppose had been watching and providing assistance to Psyche all this time? Yes, indeed, it was ol' Mama's Boy himself. He had gotten himself some therapy and decided it was time to cut the apron strings. He went straight to the board of directors on Mount Olympus and got their stamp of approval for his marriage to

Psyche. They even granted her immortality—a favor rarely given to a human. They also instructed Aphrodite to find herself a new project! With the bargain made, Cupid flew down to Psyche, wiped the sleep from her eyes and put it back in the box. Then, ever so gently, he nicked her with his arrow. (Guess he wasn't taking any chances.) He looked into her eyes and said:

Love is not love
Which alters when it alteration finds.

And Psyche smiled at him and said:

O no; it is an ever-fixed mark,
That looks on tempests, and is never shaken.[2]

And that's the way it's been from that day to this for Cupid and Psyche. ∾

---

2 passage quoted from Shakespeare's Sonnet 116

Perseus and Medusa

RICHARD WOFF

King Akrisios was a happy man. He ruled the abundant land of Argos[1] and the people of his kingdom lived in peace. His wife had died some years ago, but he had a daughter named Danaë. Her beauty and laughter filled his life with joy. She was growing up quickly and Akrisios looked forward to finding her a fine husband. He longed for the carefree embrace of grandchildren. A simple message from the gods shattered the king's hopes. On one of his visits to the temple of Apollo, the holy priestess whispered to him his terrible future: he would meet his death at the hands of his daughter's child, his own grandson.

Akrisios was desperate to avoid the death the priestess had foretold. He could not bring himself to kill Danaë, so he decided to hide her away, out of the sight of men. In spite of her tears and her pleading, he locked Danaë in a room deep underground, cut into the rock, lined with bronze, where the light of the sun never penetrated. Just one old woman was allowed to take the princess her meals. But nobody can build a barrier against Zeus. The great god had seen Danaë's loveliness. He changed himself into a shower of liquid gold and seeped into her prison to be with her. When Danaë's baby boy was born, she named him Perseus.

It is hard to hide the cries of a baby and Akrisios soon discovered Perseus. Although he realized that his life was beginning to unravel, he still could not bring himself to destroy his only family. So he ordered one of his carpenters to build a wooden box. He put Danaë and Perseus inside and nailed on the lid. Then Akrisios took the box to the shore and

---

1 **Argos:** a town as well as a region in north central Greece

set it adrift, handing over his daughter and her child to the sea. He stood and watched as the box floated to the horizon, where it was engulfed by the swell. Then he turned in sadness back to his palace.

▲ ▲ ▲

The sun's chariot had crossed the skies many times when, on the coast of the far distant island of Seriphos,[2] a fisherman hauled up a battered and salt-crusted box in his net. His heart leaped at the thought of gold and silver, but when he forced open the lid and discovered a young woman and her baby, he realized he had found an even greater treasure. He had no family, no prospect of children to care for him in his old age. The fisherman recognized from her clothes and from the glow of her loveliness that Danaë was of royal blood and could never be his wife, but he took her and Perseus into his home. The little family lived together contentedly. The fisherman cared for and respected Danaë; she learned to spin and weave and tended a small field nearby. Perseus looked after the goats and fished and mended nets. He grew into an energetic young man, strong and good looking, but he knew little of the intricate web of life.

Polydektes was the king of Seriphos. He learned of the presence of a strange woman on his island. Enticed by stories of her loveliness, he decided he had to see her for himself. As his birthday approached, Polydektes ordered all those who lived on Seriphos to come to his palace and bring him a gift. As soon as he saw Danaë, he knew he had to possess her. But her son was a problem; he would be sure to try to protect his mother. The king had to get rid of him. When it was the fisherman's turn to present his family's gift, he opened his sack and unrolled a small rush mat at the feet of the king. Then on the mat he laid out two mullet,[3] caught that very morning, their scales still gleaming silver. Next to them he placed a crumbly white cheese.

Polydektes howled with laughter. "Is that the very best that you can scrape together from your wretched little life? Is that what you think is suitable for your king? You insult me with your smelly fish and stinking cheese."

Perseus's anger flared up at once and before his mother could stop him, he cried, "If these are not good enough for you, name the gift you want. Go ahead. I will bring you anything you want."

2 **Seriphos:** island in the Aegean Sea southeast of Greece
3 **mullet:** fish valued primarily as food for other fish

Polydektes smiled. He sat back in his throne. "Far from here, in the west, where the sun god dips his chariot into the encircling river of Okeanos and brings darkness to the earth, there is a desert. The three gorgons live there. Their hair writhes with snakes, their tusks are sharper than a boar's, their wings are quicker than an eagle's. A single glimpse of a gorgon's face drains the warmth, softness and moisture of life from humans and turns them to stone. Medusa is the only gorgon of the three who can be killed. You told me to name my gift . . ." The king leaned forward, stared into the eyes of Perseus, and spoke low and calm, "Bring me the head of Medusa."

High on Olympus, Athena heard the king's words. Deep inside the goddess there still glowed an ember of resentment at Medusa for an old insult. She called to Hermes to accompany her and the two children of Zeus set off for Seriphos. They found Perseus that evening sitting at the foot of an oak tree wrapped in his cloak. He had started immediately on his search for the gorgons and was tired from a long day's walking in the heat of the sun. Athena spoke to him softly.

"Perseus, the law of my father Zeus prevents me from doing your task for you, but I can help you on your way. The Nymphs can give you three gifts which you need to win Medusa's head, but you have to find them first. Only the three ancient Graiai, the Grey Sisters, know where the Nymphs live and they will not tell you unless you force them to. Hermes will guide you to their home. Watch the sisters, watch them carefully before you do anything."

Perseus set off again with Hermes as his guide. Soon he was walking in a land of grey. The earth was a fine ash in which his feet left perfect tracks. A thick layer of smoky clouds filled the sky. Rocks lay scattered around. Their surfaces were veined with cracks and crumbled to powder at a touch. As they reached the mouth of a narrow gorge, Hermes stopped. "You will find the Grey Sisters here," he said. "Go silently and watch them." There was a sudden flutter of wings. Hermes disappeared and a sparrow darted away into the clouds.

Perseus crept forward slowly. He crouched low behind a large rock and very gradually peered around it. A little way ahead of him sat three old women. They were bundled up in thickly woven cloaks the color of cracked pepper. Their waxy skin was deeply lined and their dank hair was plastered in thick hanks over their shoulders. They were muttering and mumbling, and from time to time one would stretch out a bony arm and take something from one of the others. Perseus waited and watched.

Finally, he saw what they were doing. Instead of two eyes each, the three Graiai had just one eye between them. Instead of each sister having her own teeth, they had just one tooth between them. When one of the sisters wanted to gnaw a few crumbs from the crusts of stale bread that lay around them, she asked for the tooth and pushed it into her gums. When one of the sisters had to keep watch for trespassers, she took the eye and slipped it into one of her gaping sockets. Perseus waited and watched again. At last he saw where their weakness lay. When one of the Graiai eased the eye out of her socket and reached out to pass it to one of her sisters, for that moment, none of them could see and the eye was there for the taking. Perseus waited. Soon it was time for a change of watcher. The sister with the eye eased it from her face and held it out. Perseus darted from his hiding place and snatched the eye from the tips of her fingers.

At first each sister thought that one of the others had dropped the eye and scrabbled blindly around in the dust complaining about their carelessness. Then their frustration rose and they screamed in anger and fear. Perseus sat and watched them for a little while, enjoying his victory. Then he spoke.

"Listen to me, you hags. I am Perseus and I have what you are looking for. Tell me where I can find the Nymphs and you will have your eye back. If you refuse," he let the eyeball nestle in the palm of his hand, "I will squash the jelly out of it!" The three old women let out a howl of rage and scuttled towards the sound of Perseus' voice, but he skipped away from them with ease. "This is your last chance. Where are the Nymphs?" The sisters knew they could do nothing and told him what he wanted to know. "Thank you, ladies. Now here is your sight back," and he tossed the eye towards the women. It rolled along the ground gathering dust and grit on its sticky surface. Then he turned away and left them to their search. After he had gone some way, a cry of triumph—or was it pain?—told him they had found it.

Perseus passed out of the land of the Graiai and entered a thickly wooded valley. Here he found the Nymphs, who welcomed him graciously and gave him the three gifts Athena had mentioned. First, he pulled on a pair of winged boots, which gave him the power of flight. Second, he set on his head the helmet of death, which made him invisible and brought him under the protection of Hades. Third, he put across his shoulder a magic bag to contain Medusa's head. Finally, Hermes came to him again and gave him a hooked sword. Its keen edge was jagged like the blade of a saw. Then Hermes pointed out the way and Perseus sped off towards the land of the gorgons.

Soon he came to a desolate place. No plant grew there. Bare rock stretched away to the horizon. No river, no stream, no trickle of water slaked the thirst of the arid earth. The gods avoided this barren waste. Only the all-seeing eye of the sun gazed down on its emptiness. High above this desert, Perseus soared in the vast vault of the sky, searching for the gorgons. He found them dozing, nestled together in a sandy hollow. Athena had sent the sleep god to drip drowsiness into their eyes. Perseus hovered overhead. He was unsure which of them was the mortal Medusa, but Athena, unseen, guided his hand. Turning his face away, he stretched out his left hand and grasped Medusa's hair.

At once, a squirming mass of snakes entwined his arm. He felt his throat tighten at their disgusting touch. He raised his sword and struck. There was a gasp, almost a sob and then a long, sinking hiss. Perseus thrust the writhing head into his bag and sped away. Behind him, Medusa's headless body thrashed about and her sisters awoke. They could not see Perseus, but quickly they caught his scent and with a screech of grief and fury gave chase. They hunted Perseus across the desert and over the waters of Okeanos, but his winged boots and the guiding hand of Hermes swept him away from them.

At last, Perseus arrived back in lands where humans lived. Far below him, at the end of a rocky finger of land jutting out into the sea, he could see something moving. As he swooped down, he saw that a young woman had been chained to a rock and that a crowd of people was gathered on the nearby beach watching. At that very moment, the crowd roared out in fear and pointed out to sea. Perseus slowed down to see what was happening. Deep below the sparkling surface of the water a vast, dark shape appeared. It rose swiftly and burst from the sea in a sputtering surge of salt spray. Perseus reached into his bag, gripped Medusa's head and dived down from the sky.

The people on the beach had barely glimpsed the sea monster's enormous scaly head and its gaping jaws bearing down on their princess Andromeda, when time seemed to pause for a moment and then jerk again into motion. Suddenly, instead of a monster there was a new, misshapen rock out at sea. A young stranger was standing before their king holding Princess Andromeda's hand. Then the whole crowd cheered and wept with joy. The king embraced his daughter and announced a royal wedding and a month of rejoicing.

It was over a year later that Perseus and his wife arrived back in Seriphos. When he reached his old home, he found his mother gone and the fisherman alone. The fisherman explained that Danaë had resisted the king's desires in the hope that Perseus might return. Now she thought that her only hope was with the gods and had taken refuge at the altar of Zeus. King Polydektes and his men had surrounded her there and were starving her into submission. Perseus left Andromeda with the fisherman and taking his bag set off to find his mother.

When Polydektes saw Perseus, he mocked him. "So you are back at last. It has taken you a long time to bring my gift, but I am always happy to have a birthday present, even a late one. I suppose you have Medusa's head in that little bag. I can't say that I think much of the wrapping!" The king and his followers roared with laughter, but when Perseus drew the gorgon's head from his bag, their limbs hardened, their blood turned to sand in their veins and the laughter stopped. Then Athena came to Perseus and gently took the head from him. She was wearing her aegis skin across her chest. In its very center she set the gorgon's face to paralyze her enemies with terror and she fringed the skin with the snakes.

Perseus made the faithful fisherman king of Seriphos—he learned to be a wise king and his people grew to love him. Then, with Andromeda and Danaë, Perseus set off back to his birthplace, back to Argos to see his grandfather. When they reached Argos, Akrisios was gone. He had heard of his grandson's imminent return and had run away to escape the death the priestess had foretold. Perseus was hailed as the new king.

Some years later, in a distant land, Perseus was competing in an athletics competition. When it was his turn to throw the discus, he threw so far that the discus hit an old man in the crowd and killed him on the spot. Nobody knew the old man, so Perseus had the body brought back to Argos for burial. No one recognized the old man until Danaë came to mourn. She stood over the body and gazed down at the lifeless face of her father Akrisios. ❧

Look, Medusa!

SUNITI NAMJOSHI

Medusa lived on a remote shore
troubled no one: fish swam, birds flew, and the sea
did not turn to glass. All was as before.
A few broken statues lay untidily
on the lonely beach, but other than these
there was nothing wrong with that peaceful scene.
And so, when the hero, Perseus, came to seize
the Gorgon's head, he thought he might have been
mistaken. He watched for a while, but she turned
nothing to stone. The waves roared as waves will,
till at last the hidden hero burned
to be seen by her whom he had come to kill.
'Look, Medusa, I am Perseus!' he cried,
thus gaining recognition before he died.

RESPONDING TO CLUSTER THREE

HOW DOES MYTH EXPLAIN HUMAN NATURE?

Thinking Skill EVALUATING

1. Using a chart such as the one below, **evaluate** aspects of human nature that each selection explores. An example has been done for you.

Selection	Aspect of Human Nature
Homer, the Blind Poet	*We need to hear stories.*
Odysseus	
Siren Song	
Cupid and Psyche	
Perseus and Medusa	
Look, Medusa!	

2. Give an example of the way Odysseus solved a problem in the epic. What is another way he could have solved this problem?

3. **Hyperbole** is extreme exaggeration used for emphasis and/or humor. Find two examples in "Cupid and Psyche" that show how Barbara McBride-Smith uses hyperbole to create humor.

4. In your opinion, what is the message of "Look, Medusa!"?

Creative Activity: 'Toons

Choose a favorite scene or incident from a selection in this cluster and draw a cartoon strip that tells the story.

'Toons:

• tell a story in a series of easily understood pictures and minimal dialogue
• generally use only a few characters
• often rely on humor to make a point

CLUSTER FOUR

Thinking on Your Own
Thinking Skill SYNTHESIZING

Antaeus

BORDEN DEAL

This was during the wartime, when lots of people were coming North for jobs in factories and war industries, when people moved around a lot more than they do now and sometimes kids were thrown into new groups and new lives that were completely different from anything they had ever known before. I remember this one kid, T.J. his name was, from somewhere down South, whose family moved into our building during that time. They'd come North with everything they owned piled into the back seat of an old-model sedan that you wouldn't expect could make the trip, with T.J. and his three younger sisters riding shakily on top of the load of junk.

Our building was just like all the others there, with families crowded into a few rooms, and I guess there were twenty-five or thirty kids about my age in that one building. Of course, there were a few of us who formed a gang and ran together all the time after school, and I was the one who brought T. J. in and started the whole thing.

The building right next door to us was a factory where they made walking dolls. It was a low building with a flat, tarred roof that had a parapet[1] all around it about head high and we'd found out a long time before that no one, not even the watchman, paid any attention to the roof because it was higher than any of the other buildings around. So my gang used the roof as a headquarters. We could get up there by crossing over to the fire escape from our own roof on a plank and then going on up. It was a secret place for us, where nobody else could go without our permission.

1 **parapet:** a low wall or railing at the roof's edge

I remember the day I first took T.J. up there to meet the gang. He was a stocky, robust kid with a shock of white hair, nothing sissy about him except his voice—he talked in this slow, gentle voice, like you never heard before. He talked differently from any of us and you noticed it right away. But I liked him anyway, so I told him to come on up.

We climbed up over the parapet and dropped down on the roof. The rest of the gang were already there.

"Hi," I said. I jerked my thumb at T.J. "He just moved into the building yesterday."

He just stood there, not scared or anything, just looking, like the first time you see somebody you're not sure you're going to like.

"Hi," Blackie said. "Where are you from?"

"Marion County," T.J. said.

We laughed. "Marion County?" I said. "Where's that?"

He looked at me for a moment like I was a stranger, too. "It's in Alabama," he said, like I ought to know where it was.

"What's your name?" Charley said.

"T.J.," he said, looking back at him. He had pale blue eyes that looked washed-out but he looked directly at Charley, waiting for his reaction. He'll be all right, I thought. No sissy in him . . . except that voice. Who ever talked like that?

"T.J.," Blackie said. "That's just initials. What's your real name? Nobody in the world has just initials."

"I do," he said. "And they're T.J. That's all the name I got."

His voice was resolute with the knowledge of his rightness and for a moment no one had anything to say. T.J. looked around at the rooftop and down at the black tar under his feet. "Down yonder where I come from," he said, "we played out in the woods. Don't you-all have no woods around here?"

"Naw," Blackie said. "There's the park a few blocks over, but it's full of kids and cops and old women. You can't do a thing."

T.J. kept looking at the tar under his feet. "You mean you ain't got no fields to raise nothing in? . . . no watermelons or nothing?"

"Naw," I said scornfully. "What do you want to grow something for? The folks can buy everything they need at the store."

He looked at me again with that strange, unknowing look. "In Marion County," he said, "I had my own acre of cotton and my own acre of corn. It was mine to plant and make ever' year."

He sounded like it was something to be proud of, and in some obscure way it made the rest of us angry. "Huh!" Blackie said. "Who'd want to have their own acre of cotton and corn? That's just work. What can you do with an acre of cotton and corn?"

T.J. looked at him. "Well, you get part of the bale[2] offen your acre," he said seriously. "And I fed my acre of corn to my calf."

We didn't really know what he was talking about, so we were more puzzled than angry; otherwise, I guess, we'd have chased him off the roof and wouldn't let him be part of our gang. But he was strange and different and we were all attracted by his stolid sense of rightness and belonging, maybe by the strange softness of his voice contrasting our own tones of speech into harshness.

He moved his foot against the black tar. "We could make our own field right here," he said softly, thoughtfully. "Come spring we could raise us what we want to . . . watermelons and garden truck and no telling what all."

"You have to be a good farmer to make these tar roofs grow any water-melons," I said. We all laughed.

But T.J. looked serious. "We could haul us some dirt up here," he said. 'And spread it out even and water it and before you know it we'd have us a crop in here." He looked at us intently. "Wouldn't that be fun?"

"They wouldn't let us," Blackie said quickly.

"I thought you said this was you-all's roof," T.J. said to me. "That you-all could do anything you wanted to up here."

"They've never bothered us," I said. I felt the idea beginning to catch fire in me. It was a big idea and it took a while for it to sink in but the more I thought about it the better I liked it. "Say," I said to the gang. "He might have something there. Just make us a regular roof garden, with flowers and grass and trees and everything. And all ours, too," I said. "We wouldn't let anybody up here except the ones we wanted to."

"It'd take a while to grow trees," T.J. said quickly, but we weren't pay-ing any attention to him. They were all talking about it suddenly, all excited with the idea after I'd put it in a way they could catch hold of it. Only rich people had roof gardens, we knew, and the idea of our private domain excited them.

"We could bring it up in sacks and boxes," Blackie said. "We'd have to do it while the folks weren't paying any attention to us, for we'd have to come up to the roof of our building and then cross over with it."

---

2 **bale:** bundle of goods. Here T.J. is referring to the fact that sharecroppers get to keep some of the income from the sale of cotton.

"Where could we get the dirt?" somebody said worriedly.

"Out of those vacant lots over close to school," Blackie said. "Nobody'd notice if we scraped it up."

I slapped T.J. on the shoulder. "Man, you had a wonderful idea," I said, and everybody grinned at him, remembering that he had started it. "Our own private roof garden."

He grinned back. "It'll be ourn," he said. "All ourn." Then he looked thoughtful again. "Maybe I can lay my hands on some cotton seed, too. You think we could raise us some cotton?"

We'd started big projects before at one time or another, like any gang of kids, but they'd always petered out for lack of organization and direction. But this one didn't . . . somehow or other T.J. kept it going all through the winter months. He kept talking about the watermelons and the cotton we'd raise, come spring, and when even that wouldn't work he'd switch around to my idea of flowers and grass and trees, though he was always honest enough to add that it'd take a while to get any trees started. He always had it on his mind and he'd mention it in school, getting them lined up to carry dirt that afternoon, saying in a casual way that he reckoned a few more weeks ought to see the job through.

Our little area of private earth grew slowly. T.J. was smart enough to start in one corner of the building, heaping up the carried earth two or three feet thick, so that we had an immediate result to look at, to contemplate with awe. Some of the evenings T.J. alone was carrying earth up to the building, the rest of the gang distracted by other enterprises or interests, but T.J. kept plugging along on his own and eventually we'd all come back to him again and then our own little acre would grow more rapidly.

He was careful about the kind of dirt he'd let us carry up there and more than once he dumped a sandy load over the parapet into the areaway below because it wasn't good enough. He found out the kinds of earth in all the vacant lots for blocks around. He'd pick it up and feel it and smell it, frozen though it was sometimes, and then he'd say it was good and growing soil or it wasn't worth anything and we'd have to go on somewhere else.

Thinking about it now, I don't see how he kept us at it. It was hard work, lugging paper sacks and boxes of dirt all the way up the stairs of our own building, keeping out of the way of the grownups so they wouldn't catch on to what we were doing. They probably wouldn't have cared, for they didn't pay much attention to us, but we wanted to keep it secret anyway. Then we had to go through the trap door to our roof, teeter over a plank to the fire escape, then climb two or three stories to the parapet and drop down onto the roof. All that for a small pile of earth that sometimes didn't seem worth the effort. But T.J. kept the vision bright within us, his words shrewd and calculated toward the fulfillment of his dream; and he worked harder than any of us. He seemed driven toward a goal that we couldn't see, a particular point in time that would be definitely marked by signs and wonders that only he could see.

The laborious earth just lay there during the cold months, inert and lifeless, the clods lumpy and cold under our feet when we walked over it. But one day it rained and afterward there was a softness in the air and the earth was alive and giving again with moisture and warmth. That evening T.J. smelled the air, his nostrils dilating with the odor of the earth under his feet.

"It's spring," he said, and there was a gladness rising in his voice that filled us all with the same feeling. "It's mighty late for it, but it's spring. I'd just about decided it wasn't never gonna get here at all."

We were all sniffing at the air, too, trying to smell it the way that T.J. did, and I can still remember the sweet odor of the earth under our feet. It was the first time in my life that spring and spring earth had meant anything to me. I looked at T.J. then, knowing in a faint way the hunger within him through the toilsome winter months, knowing the dream that lay behind his plan. He was a new Antaeus,[3] preparing his own bed of strength.

"Planting time," he said. "We'll have to find us some seed."

"What do we do?" Blackie said. "How do we do it?"

"First we'll have to break up the clods," T.J. said. "That won't be hard to do. Then we plant the seed and after a while they come up. Then you got you a crop." He frowned. "But you ain't got it raised yet. You got to tend it and hoe it and take care of it and all the time it's growing and growing, while you're awake and while you're asleep. Then you lay it by when it's growed and let it ripen and then you got you a crop."

"There's those wholesale seed houses over on Sixth," I said. "We could probably swipe some grass seed over there."

T.J. looked at the earth. "You-all seem mighty set on raising some grass," he said. "I ain't never put no effort into that. I spent all my life trying not to raise grass."

"But it's pretty," Blackie said. "We could play on it and take sunbaths on it. Like having our own lawn. Lots of people got lawns."

"Well," T.J. said. He looked at the rest of us, hesitant for the first time. He kept on looking at us for a moment. "I did have it in mind to raise

---

3 **Antaeus:** mythological giant who gained his strength from Mother Earth

some corn and vegetables. But we'll plant grass."

He was smart. He knew where to give in. And I don't suppose it made any difference to him, really. He just wanted to grow something, even if it was grass.

"Of course," he said, "I do think we ought to plant a row of watermelons. They'd be mighty nice to eat while we was a-laying on that grass."

We all laughed. "All right," I said. "We'll plant us a row of watermelons."

Things went very quickly then. Perhaps half the roof was covered with the earth, the half that wasn't broken by ventilators, and we swiped pocketfuls of grass seed from the open bins in the wholesale seed house, mingling among the buyers on Saturdays and during the school lunch hour. T.J. showed us how to prepare the earth, breaking up the clods and smoothing it and sowing the grass seed. It looked rich and black now with moisture, receiving of the seed, and it seemed that the grass sprang up overnight, pale green in the early spring.

We couldn't keep from looking at it, unable to believe that we had created this delicate growth. We looked at T.J. with understanding now, knowing the fulfillment of the plan he had carried alone within his mind. We had worked without full understanding of the task but he had known all the time.

We found that we couldn't walk or play on the delicate blades, as we had expected to, but we didn't mind. It was enough just to look at it, to realize that it was the work of our own hands, and each evening the whole gang was there, trying to measure the growth that had been achieved that day.

One time a foot was placed on the plot of ground . . . one time only, Blackie stepping onto it with sudden bravado. Then he looked at the crushed blades and there was shame in his face. He did not do it again. This was his grass, too, and not to be desecrated. No one said anything, for it was not necessary.

T.J. had reserved a small section for watermelons and he was still trying to find some seed for it. The wholesale house didn't have any watermelon seed and we didn't know where we could lay our hands on them. T.J. shaped the earth into mounds, ready to receive them, three mounds lying in a straight line along the edge of the grass plot.

We had just about decided that we'd have to buy the seed if we were to get them. It was a violation of our principles, but we were anxious to get the watermelons started. Somewhere or other, T.J. got his hands on a seed catalogue and brought it one evening to our roof garden.

"We can order them now," he said, showing us the catalogue. "Look!"

We all crowded around, looking at the fat, green watermelons pictured in full color on the pages. Some of them were split open, showing the red, tempting meat, making our mouths water.

"Now we got to scrape up some seed money," T.J. said, looking at us. "I got a quarter. How much you-all got?"

We made up a couple of dollars between us and T.J. nodded his head. "That'll be more than enough. Now we got to decide what kind to get. I think them Kleckley Sweets. What do you-all think?"

He was going into esoteric matters beyond our reach. We hadn't even known there were different kinds of melons. So we just nodded our heads and agreed that Yes, we thought the Kleckley Sweets too.

"I'll order them tonight," T.J. said. "We ought to have them in a few days."

"What are you boys doing up here?" an adult voice said behind us.

It startled us, for no one had ever come up here before, in all the time we had been using the roof of the factory. We jerked around and saw three men standing near the trap door at the other end of the roof. They weren't policemen, or night watchmen, but three men in plump business suits, looking at us. They walked toward us.

"What are you boys doing up here?" the one in the middle said again.

We stood still, guilt heavy among us, levied by the tone of voice, and looked at the three strangers.

The men stared at the grass flourishing behind us. "What's this?" the man said. "How did this get up here?"

"Sure is growing good, ain't it?" T.J. said conversationally. "We planted it."

The men kept looking at the grass as if they didn't believe it. It was a thick carpet over the earth now, a patch of deep greenness startling in the sterile industrial surroundings.

"Yes sir," T.J. said proudly. "We toted that earth up here and planted that grass." He fluttered the seed catalogue. "And we're just fixing to plant us some watermelon."

The man looked at him then, his eyes strange and faraway. "What do you mean, putting this on the roof of my building?" he said. "Do you want to go to jail?"

T.J. looked shaken. The rest of us were silent, frightened by the authority of his voice. We had grown up aware of adult authority, of policemen and night watchmen and teachers, and this man sounded like all the others. But it was a new thing to T.J.

"Well, you wan't using the roof," T.J. said. He paused a moment and added shrewdly, "so we just thought to pretty it up a little bit."

"And sag it so I'd have to rebuild it," the man said sharply. He started turning away, saying to another man beside him, "See that all that junk is shoveled off by tomorrow."

"Yes sir," the man said.

T.J. started forward. "You can't do that," he said. "We toted it up here and it's our earth. We planted it and raised it and toted it up here."

The man stared at him coldly. "But it's my building," he said. "It's to be shoveled off tomorrow."

"It's our earth," T.J. said desperately. "You ain't got no right!"

The men walked on without listening and descended clumsily through the trap door. T.J. stood looking after them, his body tense with anger, until they had disappeared. They wouldn't even argue with him, wouldn't let him defend his earth-rights.

He turned to us. "We won't let 'em do it," he said fiercely. "We'll stay up here all day tomorrow and the day after that and we won't let 'em do it."

We just looked at him. We knew that there was no stopping it. He saw it in our faces and his face wavered for a moment before he gripped it into determination.

"They ain't got no right," he said. "It's our earth. It's our land. Can't nobody touch a man's own land."

We kept on looking at him, listening to the words but knowing that it was no use. The adult world had descended on us even in our richest dream and we knew there was no calculating the adult world, no fighting it, no winning against it.

We started moving slowly toward the parapet and the fire escape, avoiding a last look at the green beauty of the earth that T.J. had planted for us . . . had planted deeply in our minds as well as in our experience. We filed slowly over the edge and down the steps to the plank, T.J. coming last, and all of us could feel the weight of his grief behind us.

"Wait a minute," he said suddenly, his voice harsh with the effort of calling. We stopped and turned, held by the tone of his voice, and looked up at him standing above us on the fire escape.

"We can't stop them?" he said, looking down at us, his face strange in the dusky light. "There ain't no way to stop 'em?"

"No," Blackie said with finality. "They own the building."

We stood still for a moment, looking up at T.J., caught into inaction by the decision working in his face. He stared back at us and his face was pale in the poor light.

"They ain't gonna touch my earth," he said fiercely. "They ain't gonna lay a hand on it! Come on."

He turned around and started up the fire escape again, almost running against the effort of climbing. We followed more slowly, not knowing what he intended. By the time we reached him, he had seized a board and thrust it into the soil, scooping it up and flinging it over the parapet into the areaway below. He straightened and looked at us.

"They can't touch it," he said. "I won't let 'em lay a dirty hand on it!"

We saw it then. He stooped to his labor again and we followed, the gusts of his anger moving in frenzied labor among us as we scattered along the edge of earth, scooping it and throwing it over the parapet, destroying with anger the growth we had nurtured with such tender care. The soil carried so laboriously upward to the light and the sun cascaded swiftly into the dark areaway, the green blades of grass crumpled and twisted in the falling.

It took less time than you would think . . . the task of destruction is infinitely easier than that of creation. We stopped at the end, leaving only a scattering of loose soil, and when it was finally over a stillness stood among the group and over the factory building. We looked down at the bare sterility of black tar, felt the harsh texture of it under the soles of our shoes, and the anger had gone out of us, leaving only a sore aching in our minds like overstretched muscles.

T.J. stood for a moment, his breathing slowing from anger and effort, caught into the same contemplation of destruction as all of us. He stooped slowly, finally, and picked up a lonely blade of grass left trampled under our feet and put it between his teeth, tasting it, sucking the greenness out of it into his mouth. Then he started walking toward the fire escape, moving before any of us were ready to move, and disappeared over the edge.

We followed him but he was already halfway down to the ground, going on past the board where we crossed over, climbing down in the areaway. We saw the last section swing down with his weight and then he stood on the concrete below us, looking at the small pile of anonymous earth scattered by our throwing. Then he walked across the place where we could see him and disappeared toward the street without glancing back, without looking up to see us watching him.

They did not find him for two weeks. Then the Nashville police caught him just outside the Nashville freight yards. He was walking along the railroad track; still heading south, still heading home.

As for us, who had no remembered home to call us . . . none of us ever again climbed the escape-way to the roof. ∾

Antaeus: Looking Back at the Myth

Antaeus was a giant—and something even more than that. His father was Poseidon, the god of the sea, and his mother was the Earth herself, often known as Gaia. As you might imagine, Antaeus was extremely powerful. But he had one dire failing; he didn't know the limits of his own strength.

Whenever a stranger arrived in Antaeus' country, the giant invited him to a wrestling match. The stakes were extremely high. If Antaeus won, the stranger would be put to death, and his skull would become part of a roof Antaeus was building for a local temple.

Why anyone would accept such a challenge from a giant isn't easy to understand. Nevertheless, countless strangers did just that. Antaeus defeated them, killed them, beheaded them, and used their skulls for masonry.[1]

Antaeus emerged from every fight victorious—that is, until the hero-god Hercules came along. Like so many strangers before him, Hercules accepted Antaeus' challenge to a wrestling match. Antaeus studied Hercules' well-shaped head, secretly gloating. This skull, thought the giant, would make an especially nice addition to his temple.

Antaeus and Hercules began to fight—and right away, Hercules found himself losing. Oh, he was able to throw the giant to the ground without any trouble. But something odd kept happening when he did so. Again and again, Antaeus would rise up from the ground with greater strength than before.

Now, Hercules was never known for his great intelligence, but he was far from stupid. He quickly realized that Antaeus was drawing strength directly from the earth. The giant was, after all, the child of Gaia. It seemed that Hercules would have to reinvent the game of wrestling—or else wind up as just another ceiling ornament.

Just when he was on the verge of going down in defeat, Hercules had an idea. He seized Antaeus in his massive, brawny arms and raised him high in the air. But instead of hurling the giant to the ground, Hercules

---

1 **masonry:** building materials such as bricks or stones

simply held him aloft. Soon, Antaeus began to weaken. After the strength drained from his body, Hercules crushed him to death.

Let's not give Hercules too much credit for Antaeus' defeat. It was, after all, Antaeus' own pride and stubbornness that lifted him to his doom. And we can learn something from his example. For indeed, like Antaeus, we are all children of Mother Earth. The strength we live by comes from her. ∾

THE GIANT ANTAEUS   1861   Gustave Doré

Pegasus for a Summer

MICHAEL J. ROSEN

This is a true story about a horse. It's also a mostly true story about the horse's rider, me, but I can hardly distinguish what I remember from what I'd *like* to remember—or to forget—about myself the summer that ended as I entered seventh grade.

Outside school, I did two things better than most kids (and doing better probably meant as much to me as it meant to everyone else): swimming and horseback riding. Yet without a pool or a stable at school, I could never prove those talents to anyone. But the day camp I attended each summer provided for both.

Oh, one year, I did compete on a swim team with my best friend Johnny. I swallowed a teaspoon of honey-energy before each event with the others in my relay. All season, my eyes bore raccoon rings from the goggles. Ribbons hung from my bedroom corkboard. But I hated it, hated it just as I hated every sport that had fathers barking advice from the sidelines, or hotshot classmates divvying the rest of us into shirts and skins, or coaches always substituting in their favorite players, and team members who knew every spiteful name for someone who missed a catch, overshot a goal, slipped out of bounds, fouled, fumbled, or failed them personally in any of a zillion ways.

But I didn't give up swimming, as I had baseball, football, and basketball. (Their seasons were so brief, how could a person master one skill before everyone switched to the next sport?) And I devoted myself to horseback riding.

The whole idea of camp, which represented the whole idea of summer, hinged on those few hours each week at the camp stable, just as the whole of the school year merely anticipated the coming summer vacation. At camp, it was simply me against—against no one. It was me *with* the horse. The two of us composed the entire team, and we competed with greater opponents than just other kids. We outmaneuvered gravity, vanquished our separate fears, and mastered a third language: the wordless communication of touch and balance.

Still, I never completely lost my fear of this massive, nearly unknowable animal who was fifteen times my weight, and I don't know how many times my gawky human strength. "Keep in mind, the horse perceives *you* as the bigger animal," our riding instructor Ricki would always remind us, though not one of us believed her.

I had taken lessons from Ricki during five previous summer camps—how to read a horse's ear positions, conduct each movement with the reins, maintain posture and balance through each gait[1]—yet the only thing I remember is that I loved riding. Maybe I loved it because I excelled. Maybe I excelled because I loved it. I'd climb in the saddle, and instantly, other riders, other horses in the ring, whatever it was I didn't want to do after camp or beginning in September at junior high—it all ceased to exist, along with the rest of my life on the ground, shrinking, fading behind the trail of dust the horse and I made heading to the horizon.

Curiously, most of the obnoxious kids, the ones who did the harassing and teasing during baseball or football practice, spent their hours on horseback jerking the reins to stop their horses from munching ground clover, or thumping their boots into the sides of their uninspired horses. Not that I deliberately rode circles around them, but . . .

On those Mondays, Wednesdays, and Fridays when we rode at camp, I insisted my mother pack carrots for my lunch (for my horse—I hated carrots). I pulled on long pants and boots even when the temperature soared into the nineties. I slipped dimes in my pocket just to buy a soda in the tack room[2] after lessons. And most mornings, I bugged my favorite-counselor-of-all-time Mitch: Can I skip capture-the-flag and go help the younger kids saddle their horses? Can our group have our lunch

---

1 **gait:** manner or style of walking. Walk, trot, pace, and canter are four common gaits for horses.

2 **tack room:** part of stable where tack such as saddles and bridles are stored

at the stables? In short, can I exchange everything else camp offers for more time with the horses?

Since I was turning thirteen, this was my last summer of camp. Ricki allowed us, her senior riders, to choose our own horses. She guided us along the line of readied, haltered horses, describing each animal, hinting at its possible challenges:

"Now, Smoky, here—he's a Tennessee walker, pretty gentle, though a bit hard-mouthed. Good for one of you stronger boys. Maybe you, Allen?"

Mitch would nod in agreement, or look down the row for a more suitable match. He'd ridden most of the horses. He'd even owned a horse of his own before coming to Ohio for college.

Appaloosas, quarter horses, pintos, buckskins. Braided manes, palomino coats, legs with white stockings, faces marked with moons or stars—but really, personality was all that mattered: skittish, poky, docile, bullheaded, rascally, distracted. Some horses kicked when another horse came too close; some had to be neck-reined, others tightly reined; some wouldn't put up with a rider's mixed signals, and some, well, you couldn't always predict.

It was up to each of us to say how much spirit or obstinacy we could handle. Twenty-four riding sessions lay ahead. Almost seventy-five hours with that one chosen horse.

"Now Sparky's a girl who likes to move," Ricki said, as she swatted flies from another horse's eyes. "Used to be a jumper, too. Needs someone to keep her in check, who'd enjoy her spunk." Maybe because Ricki looked straight at me, remembering me from other summers; or maybe because of the horse's color (a flecked white coat that Ricki called "flea-bitten gray—and, no, that doesn't mean she has fleas"); or maybe because of Sparky's blue eyes that sparkled as the sun shined in (was that how she got her name?); whatever the reason, I walked right up and took Sparky's halter. Mitch gave me a quick pat on the back of my neck, which I took to be his approval.

For each riding session, we'd saddle and bridle our horses with the stable assistants' help, and then ride into the ring to practice figure eights, pivoting, cantering left and right—whatever maneuver Ricki had planned. Then it was out the gate and over a long plank bridge that spanned a marshy, spring-fed creek. As if walking a giant xylophone, the horses' hooves struck each board, and the hammered notes echoed through the hollow. Then, single file, we'd follow forest trails barely wider than a horse. Mitch would call over his shoulder to point out a horned owl's nest or the sort of tree from which baseball bats are made, or to warn us of an especially slippery embankment. Across hoof-muddied creeks, through shallow ravines, over rotting white pines and oaks, the horses performed almost without us. We simply leaned forward going under trees and backward heading down hills.

Eventually, we'd arrive at the meadow for "open practice," which mostly meant a chance to break loose. Though Ricki hadn't instructed us in any gait faster than a canter, some horses, Sparky included, just longed to gallop—it seemed more natural. Suddenly the *one, two and three, four* of her cantering hooves vanished into a lift-off, a levitation I could feel the way you can feel the instant a plane lifts off or a roller coaster dips, and I'd be weightless, hardly resting in the saddle, my heart clop-clopping its own rapid gait as I hovered at a velocity only the tears that the wind jerked from my eyes revealed. In those moments—how long did they last? No more than a minute or two—Sparky and I flew and the earth vanished entirely beneath us. She had become Pegasus, the winged Greek horse, and I, a twelve-year-old mortal, by some miracle, had been chosen to ride her.

And then, by accident, honestly, when we'd be heading back toward the barn, some horses (Sparky included) would shift from a gallop to a dead run, which, of course, was absolutely forbidden. It was too uncontrolled, too dangerous even for us advanced kids. It was too risky to allow a charging horse to stampede into the yard, careening into the barn and startling the tethered horses and the bystanders. And it was too thrilling—countless times more thrilling than anything else I'd ever experienced—to stop.

Lessons ended inside the stables, heaving loose the impossibly heavy saddle, slipping out the grassy, frothy bit, brushing and carding the horse. It meant coming down to earth and I could clearly recognize the odors: the horse's short damp hair, scratchy wool saddle blankets, the warmed worn leather, sun-parched manure, sweet hay and oats.

And finally, before leaving, I took my own reward: a bottle of orange soda from the tack room cooler.

Sparky performed like no other horse I'd ever ridden. Even Ricki told my mother on parents' night, "Those two have a special rapport." At every session, I sensed improvement. Sparky's trot smoothed out, though that probably meant I was learning to settle into her stride. She understood the instant I reined, leaned, and thumped my heel to move us into a canter. With Sparky, I finally understood what Ricki meant about how the horse and rider work in such harmony that they merge powers and thoughts to become a single creature. On the other hand, almost every lesson Ricki would pull me aside to say something like, "The two of you ought to try a little more this or that." I knew that "the two of us" actually meant the one of me.

Every day of the July Fourth week, it thundershowered and lessons had to be held indoors. The horses liked this as little as we did, but even worse, the storm distracted them, unsettled them—Sparky's ears continually flicked forward and back, fixing on whatever the wind knocked, wherever the thunder cracked.

That Friday, riding our horses into the stalls, this one kid Brett let his appaloosa named Choco drink at the trough with two other horses, though Brett knew that crowding made his horse nervous. And sure enough, another horse nosed in, and Choco bolted backward, and started bucking. The nearby horses jolted away, whinnied, and toppled a cart of straw.

"Stop, you idiot son-of-a-bitch horse!" Brett shouted in panic. (While only the counselors minded the cussing, the horses, we all knew, did not like shouting.)

"Clear out," Mitch said, as he pulled campers from the area. "Brett! Quit screaming!"

Brett hunkered down, both hands clinging to the saddle horn, both feet flopping free of the stirrups. Then Choco's hooves fired into the stall door, knocking the gate from its hinges, and Brett toppled to the floor, wedged between the wall and his spooked horse.

Mitch snatched at Choco's whipping reins, which stopped the bucking for a moment. Ricki inched along the wall to help Brett slide out of the way. Mr. Olmstead, the stable owner, appeared, too, and seized Choco's bridle, while Ricki darted in to grab Brett. But then Choco reared, trying to yank his head free, and he did, his front legs boxing in the air. But since Mitch still tugged at the reins, Choco was off-balance and heaved himself backward, battering the rear of the stall, ramming his flank right into Ricki's chest, and pinning her momentarily against the wall.

And then there was screaming—whose? Brett's, no doubt, since he'd just missed being crushed. And probably everyone else's, too, as we crowded around. Ricki slumped to the straw floor as Mr. Olmstead and Mitch yanked Choco out of the barn.

Another counselor ran to call the ambulance. The stable hands hurried the horses into stalls or out into the field to make room for the medics. Mitch treated Ricki for shock—he draped a saddle blanket over her body and pulled bits of straw from her hair. Ricki squinted from the pain. Her mouth stayed open as though trying to get the air back into her lungs. I crouched beside her and talked in a low voice, repeating over and over— *everything will be all right, the ambulance is coming, just relax*—trying to keep her from nodding off. People were always doing that on television. Our bus idled right outside the door, ready to take us home. But we were going to be late. We had to wait, find out what was going to happen. A horse had hurt not just someone, but *Ricki*. We were in a different kind of shock.

A dazed weekend ended with Mitch's announcement at flag-raising, Monday morning. "It could have been much worse. That horse could have crushed more than a few ribs. She's got four broken ribs—did you know you don't wear a cast for ribs? But it also means no riding for Ricki, and probably no camp for her."

A few of us made Ricki cards or wrote letters. Mitch gave us her address and brought stamps to camp. It turned out that she lived on the same street as my grandmother, so I biked over three days that week to visit. There were always different cars in Ricki's driveway, so I'd ride over to Grandma's and have one of her ice-cream floats, then ride around the block a few more times, and then, convinced that Ricki was busy and didn't really want camp kids bothering her, race home for dinner. I also thought I'd tell my parents I wanted to stop going to camp; I circled that topic for three days as well, before dropping it.

The owner's youngest son, Gibby, took over for Ricki. We sort of knew him—he was the one who slapped the horses' rears to move them in or out of their stalls. Gibby didn't know our names. He didn't bother to use the horses' names. For three straight sessions, Gibby had us circle him in the ring while he pelted dirt clods at the horses that weren't keeping in step, until the time ran out.

Then someone besides us kids must have complained, because with only a few sessions left, Gibby brought out his own horse, Striker, told us to march behind him "in a perfectly straight line, one horse's-length apart," and led us to the meadow.

"You're on your own," he said. "Just don't run 'em." Then he dismounted and gathered dirt clods.

Mitch and I and a few other kids turned our horses away from the group, just as Gibby called out to someone, "Keep that blind mare to a trot." I leaned into a canter, and Sparky responded as though she, too, had been waiting for free practice. Behind us, Gibby shouted his warning again: "I said, don't race her. Take the field at a trot."

Just as I completed one half-circle, passing Mitch on his horse Paintbrush, a dirt clod whizzed past my chest. "You, for crying out loud! Listen to me!"

"You want me?" I called back as I jerked the reins to bring Sparky to a halt. Horses crisscrossed the field between Gibby and me.

"No, I want to talk to myself all day!" he shouted, even though he'd come close enough to just talk. "Yes, you. Too many holes and burrows to be running a blind animal! Trot her. Got it? Trot."

"What do you mean? Sparky's not blind."

"Right. *She's* not blind, and *you're* not stupid. Look, kid, just keep it slow, got it?" And then Gibby turned to yell at another kid who'd dropped his reins over his horse's grazing head.

I hopped down and stood in front of Sparky. Her enormous eyes gazed to each side, blinking, wondering, no doubt, why we weren't flying, what I was doing on the ground. I moved to stare into her right eye, at the sun breaking from clouds that were as much in her eye as in the sky. And I shuffled over and stared into her left eye, at the herd of tiny horses and riders veering toward the woods. I pressed my face to her velvet muzzle, and I held my breath, trying not to cry, trying not to let my eyes water or my breath leak even a sob, but I couldn't. How many times had Sparky walked me through those woods, never once stumbling as she lifted her hooves across the gullies and rotting trees? She had always dodged slower horses and obstacles in the ring. She recognized me. Even Ricki said she did. A blind horse could do all that?

Before long, Mitch came to see what was wrong. I shook my head to answer his questions. *No*, I wasn't hurt. *No*, I wasn't scared. *No*, nothing happened. *No*, I'm not going to just hop on and ride on home. *No*, I don't care if the other kids see me crying. Ultimately, I said that I hated Gibby, I hated him, I hated camp, and everything else because how could I like anything if, if Sparky was blind! If the whole world was this unfair! Blind? How could I not have known that? Seen that? Felt that? Gibby was right: I was stupid—*and I was blind.*

I wanted to stand in that field and I wanted to cry at least until camp ended, and maybe until summer ended, and maybe until I turned thirteen or nineteen or thirty and this sadness, this overpoweringly sorry feeling—about Sparky, about myself—had run dry like the tears.

But it didn't take that long. The bus was waiting back at the stables. "Come on, I'll help you up," Mitch said and cupped his hands beside the stirrup as though I'd ever needed a boost from him or anyone else. I took Sparky's reins and led her across the field and into the woods, retracing a path that my own two feet had never before touched.

The next week, my last week of camp, Ricki felt well enough to return. Laughing made her chest hurt, and so did talking loud, so she couldn't do more than sit outside the ring and watch us perform for her final evaluation.

I packed carrots for Sparky and sugar cubes and every apple we had in our fruit bin. I didn't know how else to say good-bye. Instead of watching the other campers execute the set routine that Ricki had rehearsed with us, I brushed Sparky until her coat gleamed and Mitch called for the *R*s in the alphabet of camper names. And then Sparky and I executed the specified maneuvers because, really, they only required my two eyes and her four legs. She didn't fidget in place when I lifted each of her hooves, removed the halter and bridled her, mounted, dismounted, and then mounted again. She both walked and trotted in figure eights along the flagged poles, never brushing a single one. Sparky backed up, turned circles, left and right, cantered at the first signal, and stopped exactly alongside Ricki in the bleachers. I didn't have to ask her twice to do anything. And yet, instead of being pleased or proud, I felt only relief as I dismounted. How could I ride Sparky as though her blindness didn't matter?

On Friday, after the awards in boating and camp crafts and nature studies, Ricki presented her awards. The newer kids became Colts; some attained Yearling status; and some of the advanced riders, Thoroughbred. Moving very slowly, Ricki presented each of us a certificate and a card for a wallet, which, of course, none of us had. Maybe because I already had two Thoroughbred cards from previous summers, Ricki left me out of the roll.

Then Ricki returned to her seat, gathered her backpack, and walked over, maybe to explain. But when she stood in front of me, instead of a whisper she announced, "This year, we have a special achievement honor, The Pegasus Award . . ." My heart beat so loudly I couldn't hear any of her words, let alone my name. As Ricki pressed a blue-ribboned card and a small trophy of a winged horse into my hands, I heard her say, "Just don't hug me. Congratulations!" I couldn't keep my eyes from filling with tears again, the happy kind, at least in part. The clapping grew loud, like the horse hooves echoing from the planks of our ravine bridge.

"Ricki," I forced myself to say her name. "Ricki, did you know that Sparky is blind?"

"Of course, yes."

"But—but *I* didn't. I cantered all those days in the field, and she could have fallen in the, in the holes, and Gibby—"

"Any horse can fall. But most always, they don't. You're a good rider, a careful one, and Sparky's eyesight is just about as important as her saddle color when it comes to riding. But . . . well . . . maybe I should have pointed that out."

The applause had stopped by now, and Mitch, crouching behind my knees, had pulled me onto his shoulders and stood.

"Bravo, Pegasus!" he exclaimed, while the other kids in my group leaped up to smack my butt as though I'd scored the final point in some important game.

Before we left the stables, I went to Sparky's stall. Under the dim overhead bulb, I waved my hands in front of one eye, then the other. Her ears flickered with attention. Her nostrils flared as they gathered a scent she clearly recognized. What did I expect to see? Each wide-open eye had any other horse's gaze.

And that was it. I never saw Sparky again. I never rode another horse. As for Ricki and Mitch, and even some of my friends from that day camp—they, too, remain within that one particular summer.

Curiously, it's Gibby I continue to see. Not in person, but when I obsess about the cruel things that seem so natural to us as people—cruelties to animals, including our own kind—it's Gibby, just a blurry image of him that reappears, shouting the word "stupid," and firing dirt clods.

One other thing does reappear every now and then. This image of myself, stunned and weeping in the middle of that meadow. And while that twelve-year-old boy and, no doubt, that mythic horse, are long gone, I now can see—rather than the sun, woods, or other riders—my own reflection in that cloudy, uncomprehending, sparkling eye of my horse. It's not so different from who I am today. ∾

Pegasus: Looking Back at the Myth

Whenever hearts soar and spirits fly, whenever the stomp of earthbound hooves gives way to the rustle of wings, there is Pegasus. The magnificent flying horse with huge white wings lives not in the stables and meadows of earth but on the updrafts of the wind and the imagination.

Like so many other creatures of Greek mythology, Pegasus was not born in the usual way. He sprang full-grown from the blood of Medusa, a hideous she-monster with snakes for hair—a creature so fearsome that the mere sight of her turned men to stone. When the hero Perseus chopped off Medusa's head, Pegasus was born.

But thereby hangs a tale for another telling. The important thing is that the winged horse came to be. He stampeded through the world until the goddess Athena found and tamed him. All the gods took great delight in him—especially the Muses, the nine sister goddesses of song and memory. Pegasus returned their affection by stomping his hooves on the mountain where the Muses lived, making waters arise into a sacred spring.

But no one rode the skittish Pegasus—not until a daring young man named Bellerophon glimpsed the fabulous beast and set his heart on the flying horse. Knowing that Athena was the creature's friend, Bellerophon prayed all night in her temple.

Athena was moved by Bellerophon's prayers and presented him with a golden bridle. Then she guided him to where Pegasus could be found— drinking at a well. Bellerophon gently put the bridle on the winged horse. At that moment, Pegasus became his to ride.

Bellerophon rode Pegasus to glory. Flying high in the air on Pegasus' back, he shot a fatal arrow at the fearsome Chimaera—a fire-breathing monster with a lion's head, a goat's body, and serpent for a tail. With Pegasus' help, Bellerophon became a hero. He warred victoriously against whole armies—including the Amazons, a mighty race of women warriors.

But Bellerophon's pride and ambition finally got the best of him. He tried to ride Pegasus to the heights of Mount Olympus in hopes of becoming an immortal god. Zeus, the father of the gods, was most displeased, and sent a biting fly to sting Pegasus. Bucking and rearing in the heavens, the startled horse accidentally threw his master from his back. Bellerophon plummeted to the ground, his bones splintering with the force of impact. Humbled, lame and blind, the fallen hero wandered the earth for the rest of his days.

Pegasus still soars through the dreams of adventurers. But those who long to tame him with a golden bridle should be careful where they ride. Mortals are not welcome on the heights of Olympus. ∾

BELLEROPHON ON PEGASUS   Walter Crane

Phoenix Farm

JANE YOLEN

We moved into Grandma's farm right after our apartment house burned down along with most of the neighborhood. Even without the fire, it had not been a good California summer, dry as popcorn and twice as salty, what with all the sweat running down our faces.

I didn't mind so much—the fire, I mean. I had hated that apartment, with its pockmarked walls and the gang names scribbled on the stoop. Under my bedroom window someone had painted the words "Someday, sugar, you gonna find no one in this world gonna give you sweet." The grammar bothered me more than what it said.

Mama cried, though. About the photos, mostly. And about all her shoes having burned up. She has real tiny feet and her one vanity is shoes. She can buy the model stuff for really cheap. But it's not just the photos and the shoes. She cries about everything these days. It's been that way since Daddy died.

Ran off. That's what Nicky says. A week before the fire. *Couldn't take it. The recession and all. No job. No hope.*

Mama says it won't be forever, but I say he died. I can deal with it that way.

And besides, we don't want him back.

So we got ready to head for Grandma's farm up in the valley, with only the clothes we'd been wearing; our cat, Tambourine; and Mama's track medals, all fused together. She found them when the firefighters let us go back upstairs to sort through things. Nicky grabbed a souvenir, too. His old basketball. It was flat and blackened, like a pancake someone left on the stove too long.

I looked around and there was nothing I wanted to take. Nothing. All that I cared about had made it through the fire: Mama, Nicky, and Tam. It was as if we could start afresh and all the rest of it had been burned away. But as we were going down the stairs—the iron stairs, not the wooden ones inside, which were all gone—I saw the most surprising thing. On the thirteenth step up from the bottom, tucked against the riser, was a nest. It was unburnt, unmarked, the straw that held it the rubbed-off gold of a wheat field. A piece of red string ran through it, almost as if it had been woven on a loom. In the nest was a single egg.

It didn't look like any egg I'd ever seen before, not dull white or tan like the eggs from the store. Not even a light blue like the robin's egg I'd found the one summer we'd spent with Grandma at the farm. This was a shiny, shimmery gray-green egg with a red vein—the red thread—cutting it in half.

"Look!" I called out. But Mama and Nicky were already in the car, waiting. So without thinking it all the way through—like, what was I going to do with an egg, and what about the egg's mother, and what if it broke in the car or, worse, hatched—I picked it up and stuck it in the pocket of my jacket. Then, on second thought, I took off the jacket and made a kind of nest of it, and carefully carried the egg and my jacket down the rest of the stairs.

When I got into the car, it was the very first time I had ever ridden in the back all alone without complaining. And all the way to the farm, I kept the jacket-nest and its egg in my lap. All the way.

Grandma welcomed us, saying, "I'm not surprised. Didn't I tell you?" Meaning that Daddy wasn't with us. She and Mama didn't fight over it, which was a surprise on its own. Neighbors of Grandma's had collected clothes for us. It made us feel like refugees, which is an awkward feeling that makes you prickly and cranky most of the time. At least that's how I felt until I found a green sweater that exactly matches my eyes and Nicky found a Grateful Dead T-shirt. There were no shoes Mama's size. And no jobs nearby, either.

I stashed the egg in its jacket-nest on the dresser Mama and I shared. Nicky, being the only boy, got his own room. Mama never said a word about the egg. It was like she didn't even see it. I worried what she'd say if it began to smell.

But the days went by and the egg never did begin to stink. We got settled into our new school. I only thought about Daddy every *other* day.

And I found a best friend right away. Nicky had girls calling him after dinner for the first time. So we were OK.

Mama wasn't happy, though. She and Grandma didn't exactly quarrel, but they didn't exactly get along, either. Being thankful to someone doesn't make you like them. And since Mama couldn't find a job, they were together all day long.

Then one evening my new best friend, Ann Marie, was over. We were doing homework together up in my room. It was one of those coolish evenings and the windows were closed, but it was still pretty bright outside, considering.

Ann Marie suddenly said, "Look! Your egg is cracking open."

I looked up and she was right. We hadn't noticed anything before, because the crack had run along the red line. When I put my finger on the crack, it seemed to pulse.

"Feel that!" I said.

Ann Marie touched it, then jerked back as if she had been burned. "I'm going home now," she said.

"But, Ann Marie, aren't you the one who dragged me to see all those horror movies and—"

"Movies aren't real," she said. She grabbed up her books and ran from the room.

I didn't even say good-bye. The egg had all my attention, for the gray-green shell seemed to be taking little breaths, pulsing in and out, in and out, like a tiny brittle ocean. Then the crack widened, and as if there were a lamp inside, light poured out.

Nicky came in then, looking for some change on the dresser.

"Neat!" he said when he saw the light. "Do you know what kind of bird it's going to be? Did you look it up in Dad—" And then he stopped, because all of Daddy's books had been burned up. Besides, we didn't mention him anymore. And since we hadn't heard from him at all, it was like he really *was* dead.

"No," I said. "And I don't think it's any *ordinary* bird that you would find in an *ordinary* book."

"A lizard, you think?"

Never taking my eyes off the egg, I shook my head. How stupid could he be? With that light coming out? A dragon, maybe. Then the phone rang downstairs and he ran out of the room, expecting, I guess, that it would be Courtney or Brittany or another of his girlfriends named after spaniels. Talking to them was more important to him than my egg.

But I continued to watch. I was the only one watching when it hatched. How such a large bird got into such a small egg, I'll never know. But that's magic for you. It rose slowly out of the egg, pushing the top part of the shell with its golden head. Its beak was golden, too, and curved like one of those Arabian swords. Its eyes were hooded and dark, without a center. When it stared at me, I felt drawn in.

The bird gave a sudden kind of shudder and humped itself farther out of the egg, and its wings were blue and scarlet and gold, all shimmery, like some seashells when they're wet. It shook out its wings, and they were wide enough to touch from one side of the dresser to the other, the individual feathers throwing off sparkles of light.

Another shudder, and the bird stood free of the egg entirely, though a piece of shell still clung to the tip of one wing. I reached over and freed it, and it seared my fingers—the touch of the feather, not the shell. The bird's scarlet body and scaly golden feet pulsed with some kind of heat.

"What *are* you?" I whispered, then stuck my burnt fingers in my mouth to soothe them.

If the bird could answer me, it didn't; it just pumped its wings, which seemed to grow wider with each beat. The wind from them was a Santa Ana, hot and heavy and thick.

I ran to the window and flung it wide, holding the curtain aside.

The bird didn't seem to notice my effort, but still it flew unerringly outside. I saw it land once on a fencepost; a second time, on the roof of Grandma's barn. Then it headed straight toward the city, the setting sun making a fire in its feathers.

When I couldn't see it anymore, I turned around. The room smelled odd—like the ashes of a fire, but like something else, too. Cinnamon, maybe. Or cloves.

I heard the doorbell. It rang once, then a second time. Grandma and Mama were off visiting a neighbor. Nicky was still on the phone. I ran down the stairs and flung the door wide open.

Daddy was standing there, a new beard on his face and a great big Madame Alexander doll in his arms.

"I got a job, baby. In Phoenix. And a house rented. With a real back-yard. I didn't know about the fire, I didn't know where you all had gone. My letters came back and the phone didn't connect and . . ."

"Daddy!" I shouted, and he dropped the box to scoop me up against his chest. As I snuggled my face against his neck, I smelled that same smell: ashes and cinnamon, maybe cloves. Where my burnt fingers tangled in his hair they hurt horribly.

Grandma would be furious. Nicky and Mama might be, too. But I didn't care. There's dead. And there's not.

Sometimes it's better to rise up out of the ashes, singing. ❧

Phoenix: Looking Back at the Myth

In Greek mythology, a large, brilliantly feathered bird called the Phoenix was a symbol of hope, rebirth, and immortality. Today scholars believe that the Greeks may have taken the idea of the Phoenix from the Egyptian *benu*, also a large bird. Similar to a stork, it was considered sacred.

The bird in both cultures represented the sun, which goes down in flames every evening only to reemerge each dawn. When the city of Phoenix, Arizona, was established in the 1860s, it was so named because an ancient Indian civilization had once thrived on the same site.

The Greeks and the Egyptians weren't the only cultures to share a similar myth. Myths, particularly nature myths, travel widely from place to place and age to age.

In the Greek version of this myth, only one Phoenix existed at any one time. With a body larger than an eagle, the Phoenix commanded the skies. It was always male and lived for consecutive life spans of 500 years.

Unlike creatures earthbound and ordinary, the Phoenix was not born of others but had the magical ability to reproduce itself. At the end of its long life cycle, it flew to its doom at the top of an oak or palm tree, where it began to build the nest in which it would die.

First the bird would sweeten its death nest with exotic spices and resins such as cinnamon and myrrh. On top of this fragrant pile of twigs and branches, the Phoenix built the funeral pyre on which it would breathe its last breath before burning itself to death. After it died, the remains of the smoldering body were enclosed in an egg made of myrrh. From this egg, the young Phoenix hatched. The fledgling bird then rose from the ashes, grew strong, and soared. Like its parent, the new Phoenix was destined to live its own 500 years.

Once it could take flight, the young bird's duty was to deliver its father's remains to the altar of the sun god in the Egyptian city of Heliopolis, City of the Sun. There the father bird's remnants were consumed in a cleansing fire.

Today, poets refer to the Phoenix as both male and female. Its spirit is perhaps best expressed by the poet Emily Dickinson, who wrote, "Hope is the thing with feathers that perches in the soul." ∾

MOSAIC PAVEMENT FROM THE COURTYARD OF A VILLA AT DAPHNE
Circa 500 B.C.

*In Greek mythology, Icarus was imprisoned on a closely
guarded island with his father Daedalus, who devised an escape
plan inspired by watching the seagulls circling above. Deciding
that the sky was their only avenue of escape, Daedalus constructed
wings of feathers secured with wax so he and his son could fly to
freedom. Despite his father's warning to fly at a moderate height,
Icarus grew bold and flew too close to the sun. When the sun
melted the wax on his wings, he fell to his death in the sea.*

I, Icarus

ALDEN NOWLAN

There was a time when I could fly. I swear it.
Perhaps, if I think hard for a moment, I can even tell you the
    year.
My room was on the ground floor at the rear of the house.
My bed faced a window.
Night after night I lay on my bed and willed myself to fly.
It was hard work, I can tell you.
Sometimes I lay perfectly still for an hour before I felt
    my body rising from the bed.
I rose slowly, slowly until I floated three or four feet
    above the floor.
Then with a kind of swimming motion, I propelled myself toward the
    window.
Outside, I rose higher and higher, above the pasture fence,
    above the clothesline, above the dark, haunted trees
    beyond the pasture.
And, all the time, I heard the music of flutes.
It seemed the wind made this music.
And sometimes there were voices singing.

ICARUS, FROM "JAZZ"
1943
Henri Matisse

A Whole Nation and a People

HARRY MARK PETRAKIS

There was one storekeeper I remember above all others in my youth. It was shortly before I became ill, spending a good portion of my time with a motley group of varied ethnic ancestry. We contended with one another to deride the customs of the old country. On our Saturday forays into neighborhoods beyond our own, to prove we were really Americans, we ate hot dogs and drank Cokes. If a boy didn't have ten cents for this repast he went hungry, for he dared not bring a sandwich from home made of the spiced meats our families ate.

One of our untamed games was to seek out the owner of a pushcart or a store, unmistakably an immigrant, and bedevil him with a chorus of insults and jeers. To prove allegiance to the gang it was necessary to reserve our fiercest malevolence[1] for a storekeeper or peddler belonging to our own ethnic background.

For that reason I led a raid on the small, shabby grocery of old Barba Nikos, a short, sinewy Greek who walked with a slight limp and sported a flaring, handlebar mustache.

We stood outside his store and dared him to come out. When he emerged to do battle, we plucked a few plums and peaches from the baskets on the sidewalk and retreated across the street to eat them while he watched. He waved a fist and hurled epithets[2] at us in ornamental Greek.

Aware that my mettle[3] was being tested, I raised my arm and threw my half-eaten plum at the old man. My aim was accurate and the plum

---

1 **malevolence:** ill will; hatred
2 **epithets:** names or curses
3 **mettle:** courage

struck him on the cheek. He shuddered and put his hand to the stain. He stared at me across the street, and although I could not see his eyes, I felt them sear my flesh. He turned and walked silently back into the store. The boys slapped my shoulders in admiration, but it was a hollow victory that rested like a stone in the pit of my stomach.

At twilight, when we disbanded, I passed the grocery alone on my way home. There was a small light burning in the store and the shadow of the old man's body outlined against the glass. Goaded by remorse, I walked to the door and entered.

The old man moved from behind the narrow wooden counter and stared at me. I wanted to turn and flee, but by then it was too late. As he motioned for me to come closer, I braced myself for a curse or a blow.

"You were the one," he said, finally, in a harsh voice.

I nodded mutely.

"Why did you come back?"

I stood there unable to answer.

"What's your name?"

"Haralambos," I said, speaking to him in Greek.

He looked at me in shock. "You are Greek!" he cried. "A Greek boy attacking a Greek grocer!" He stood appalled at the immensity of my crime. "All right," he said coldly. "You are here because you wish to make amends." His great mustache bristled in concentration. "Four plums, two peaches," he said. "That makes a total of seventy-eight cents. Call it seventy-five. Do you have seventy-five cents, boy?"

I shook my head.

"Then you will work it off," he said. "Fifteen cents an hour into seventy-five cents makes"—he paused—"five hours of work. Can you come here Saturday morning?"

"Yes," I said.

"Yes, Barba Nikos," he said sternly. "Show respect."

"Yes, Barba Nikos," I said.

"Saturday morning at eight o'clock," he said. "Now go home and say thanks in your prayers that I did not loosen your impudent head with a solid smack on the ear." I needed no further urging and fled.

Saturday morning, still apprehensive, I returned to the store. I began by sweeping, raising clouds of dust in dark and hidden corners. I washed the windows, whipping the squeegee swiftly up and down the glass in a fever of fear that some member of the gang would see me. When I finished I hurried back inside.

For the balance of the morning I stacked cans, washed the counter, and dusted bottles of yellow wine. A few customers entered, and Barba Nikos served them. A little after twelve o'clock he locked the door so he could eat lunch. He cut himself a few slices of sausage, tore a large chunk from a loaf of crisp-crusted bread, and filled a small cup with a dozen black shiny olives floating in brine.[4] He offered me the cup. I could not help myself and grimaced.

"You are a stupid boy," the old man said. "You are not really Greek, are you?"

"Yes, I am."

"You might be," he admitted grudgingly. "But you do not act Greek. Wrinkling your nose at these fine olives. Look around this store for a minute. What do you see?"

"Fruits and vegetables," I said. "Cheese and olives and things like that."

He stared at me with a massive scorn. "That's what I mean," he said. "You are a bonehead. You don't understand that a whole nation and a people are in this store."

I looked uneasily toward the storeroom in the rear, almost expecting someone to emerge.

"What about olives?" he cut the air with a sweep of his arm. "There are olives of many shapes and colors. Pointed black ones from Kalamata, oval ones from Amphissa, pickled green olives and sharp tangy yellow ones. Achilles carried black olives to Troy and after a day of savage battle leading his Myrmidons, he'd rest and eat cheese and ripe black olives such as these right here. You have heard of Achilles, boy, haven't you?"

"Yes," I said.

"Yes, Barba Nikos."

"Yes, Barba Nikos," I said.

He motioned at the rows of jars filled with varied spices. "There is origanon there and basilikon and daphne and sesame and miantanos, all the marvelous flavorings that we have used in our food for thousands of years. The men of Marathon carried small packets of these spices into battle, and the scents reminded them of their homes, their families, and their children."

He rose and tugged his napkin free from around his throat. "Cheese, you said. Cheese! Come closer, boy, and I will educate your abysmal

4 **brine:** salty water used to flavor and preserve food

ignorance." He motioned toward a wooden container on the counter. "That glistening white delight is feta, made from goat's milk, packed in wooden buckets to retain the flavor. Alexander the Great demanded it on his table with his casks of wine when he planned his campaigns."

He walked limping from the counter to the window where the piles of tomatoes, celery, and green peppers clustered. "I suppose all you see here are some random vegetables?" He did not wait for me to answer. "You are dumb again. These are some of the ingredients that go to make up a Greek salad. Do you know what a Greek salad really is? A meal in itself, an experience, an emotional involvement. It is created deftly and with grace. First, you place large lettuce leaves in a big, deep bowl." He spread his fingers and moved them slowly, carefully, as if he were arranging the leaves. "The remainder of the lettuce is shredded and piled in a small mound," he said. "Then comes celery, cucumbers, tomatoes sliced lengthwise, green peppers, origanon, green olives, feta, avocado, and anchovies. At the end you dress it with lemon, vinegar, and pure olive oil, glinting golden in the light."

He finished with a heartfelt sigh and for a moment closed his eyes. Then he opened one eye to mark me with a baleful intensity. "The story goes that Zeus himself created the recipe and assembled and mixed the ingredients on Mount Olympus one night when he had invited some of the other gods to dinner."

He turned his back on me and walked slowly again across the store, dragging one foot slightly behind him. I looked uneasily at the clock, which showed that it was a few minutes past one. He turned quickly and startled me. "And everything else in here," he said loudly. "White beans, lentils, garlic, crisp bread, kokoretsi, meatballs, mussels and clams." He paused and drew a deep, long breath. "And the wine," he went on, "wine from Samos, Santorini, and Crete, retsina and mavrodaphne, a taste almost as old as water . . . and then the fragrant melons, the pastries, yellow diples and golden loukoumades, the honey custard galatobouriko. Everything a part of our history, as much a part as the exquisite sculpture in marble, the bearded warriors, Pan and the oracles at Delphi, and the nymphs dancing in the shadowed groves under Homer's glittering moon." He paused, out of breath again, and coughed harshly. "Do you understand now, boy?"

He watched my face for some response and then grunted. We stood silent for a moment until he cocked his head and stared at the clock. "It is time for you to leave," he motioned brusquely toward the door. "We are square now. Keep it that way."

I decided the old man was crazy and reached behind the counter for my jacket and cap and started for the door. He called me back. From a box he drew out several soft, yellow figs that he placed in a piece of paper. "A bonus because you worked well," he said. "Take them. When you taste them, maybe you will understand what I have been talking about."

I took the figs and he unlocked the door and I hurried from the store. I looked back once and saw him standing in the doorway, watching me, the swirling tendrils of food curling like mist about his head.

I ate the figs late that night. I forgot about them until I was in bed, and then I rose and took the package from my jacket. I nibbled at one, then ate them all. They broke apart between my teeth with a tangy nectar, a thick sweetness running like honey across my tongue and into the pockets of my cheeks. In the morning when I woke, I could still taste and inhale their fragrance.

I never again entered Barba Nikos' store. My spell of illness, which began some months later, lasted two years. When I returned to the streets I had forgotten the old man and the grocery. Shortly afterwards my family moved from the neighborhood.

Some twelve years later, after the war, I drove through the old neighborhood and passed the grocery. I stopped the car and for a moment stood before the store. The windows were stained with dust and grime, the interior bare and desolate, a store in a decrepit group of stores marked for razing so new structures could be built.

▲ ▲ ▲

I have been in many Greek groceries since then and have often bought the feta and Kalamata olives. I have eaten countless Greek salads and have indeed found them a meal for the gods. On the holidays in our house, my wife and sons and I sit down to a dinner of steaming, buttered pilaf like my mother used to make and lemon-egg avgolemono and roast lamb richly seasoned with cloves of garlic. I drink the red and yellow wines, and for dessert I have come to relish the delicate pastries coated with honey and powdered sugar. Old Barba Nikos would have been pleased.

But I have never been able to recapture the halcyon flavor of those figs he gave me on that day so long ago, although I have bought figs many times. I have found them pleasant to my tongue, but there is something missing. And to this day I am not sure whether it was the figs or the vision and passion of the old grocer that coated the fruit so sweetly I can still recall their savor and fragrance after almost thirty years. ∾

RESPONDING TO CLUSTER FOUR

Thinking Skill SYNTHESIZING

1. Each of the other clusters in this book is introduced by a question that is meant to help readers focus their thinking about the selections. What do you think the question for Cluster Four should be?

2. How do you think the selections in this cluster should be taught? Demonstrate your ideas by joining with your classmates to

   - create discussion questions.
   - lead discussions about the selections.
   - develop vocabulary activities.
   - prepare a cluster quiz.

REFLECTING ON *ECHOES FROM MT. OLYMPUS*

Essential Question WHY DOES MYTH ENDURE?

Reflecting on this book as a whole provides an opportunity for independent learning and the application of the critical thinking skill, synthesis. *Synthesizing* means examining all the things you have learned from this book and combining them to form a richer and more meaningful view of why myths have endured.

There are many ways to demonstrate what you know about mythology. Here are some possibilities. Your teacher may provide others.

1. After reading this book, you should have a better idea of what a myth is. Pretend you are trying to communicate the meaning of the word "mythology" with a foreign student just learning English. Without looking at any resources, write a clear definition for this term. Share your result with your class.

2. Individually or in small groups, develop an independent project that demonstrates what you have learned about mythology. For example, you might give an oral presentation about the influences of mythology on our culture. Other options might include a music video, dance, poem, performance, drama, or artistic rendering.

CLOSE READING

Re-reading, we find a new book. —Mason Cooley

Close reading is the careful interpretation of a text. Re-reading is the key strategy for close reading. The "new book" readers often encounter on re-reading is layered with meaning.

There is no single right way to do a close reading of a text. The following general process, however, presents three broad stages or levels in re-reading that build on one another to help produce a deep understanding of a text.

1. First Readings: Build Understanding

On a first reading, focus on grasping the literal or explicit meaning of a text. Answer the questions as you read, paraphrase key ideas, and jot down any questions you have.

Informational Text	
Questions to Ask	**Where to Look for Answers**
What is the main idea?	Title, introduction, or first few paragraphs
What information backs up the main idea?	Body paragraphs, especially their topic sentences
How are the ideas in the text related to one another?	Transitions between sections/ideas
What conclusion does the writer draw, and how does it relate to the main idea and supporting ideas?	Concluding paragraphs

Argumentative Text	
Questions to Ask	**Where to Look for Answers**
What is the main claim, or point the writer is trying to prove?	Title, introduction, or first few paragraphs
What evidence does the writer provide to back up that claim?	Body paragraphs, especially their topic sentences
What counterclaims, if any, does the writer address?	Body paragraphs, often marked with such words and phrases as "in contrast," "despite," "while it is true that"
How are the ideas in the text related to one another?	Transitions between sections/ideas
What conclusion does the writer draw, and how does it relate to the main claim and supporting ideas?	Concluding paragraphs

Narrative Text	
Questions to Ask	**Where to Look for Answers**
What event starts the narrative in motion?	Introduction or first few paragraphs
What is the setting of the narrative?	Introduction and throughout
Who are the people or characters in the narrative?	Introduction and throughout
What problem do the people or characters face?	Introduction and throughout
What happens to the people or characters as the narrative unfolds?	Body paragraphs
What is the outcome or resolution of the narrative?	Concluding paragraphs

Poetry	
Questions to Ask	**Where to Look for Answers**
If the poem tells a story, what is the basic outline of that story?	Throughout
What is the tone of the poem?	Throughout
What images, words, or ideas stand out as striking?	Throughout
What images, words, or ideas are repeated, if any?	Throughout
What message do you see in the poem?	Title, throughout

2. Focused Re-readings: Analyze the Text and Gather Evidence

Re-reading after you have grasped a basic understanding of a text is the stage at which you are most likely to encounter that "new book" referred to in the beginning quote, because at this level you analyze the text carefully and focus on details that may bring new meaning to what you have read. The chart below shows some of the points you can focus on in a re-reading of almost any kind of text. It also shows what questions you can ask and where and how you can discover the answers to those questions.

Focused Re-reading		
Focus and Thinking Skills	**Questions to Ask**	**Finding Textual Evidence**
Author's purpose, such as to inform, put forward an argument, entertain, satirize, tell a story *Thinking skills: Recognize explicit statements; draw inferences about implied purpose(s)*	Why did the writer write this? Is the purpose stated explicitly or is it only implied?	Look in the title and beginning paragraphs for quotes that show the answers to your questions.

continued

Focus and Thinking Skills	Questions to Ask	Finding Textual Evidence
Word choice and style, including length of sentences, variety of sentence beginnings, and variety of sentence types *Thinking skills: Analyze; break passages down by word choice and sentence style and look for patterns*	What words and phrases caught your attention for their strength and clarity? Does the author tend to use long sentences, short sentences, or a variety of sentence lengths? Do the sentences begin in a variety of ways (for example, subject first, prepositional phrase first, etc.)?	Look throughout for examples that demonstrate the results of your analysis (for example, three vivid word choices, three varied sentence patterns, etc.). In a long text, examine a section from the beginning, two or three sections from the middle, and a section from the end.
Figurative language, such as similes, metaphors, hyperbole, alliteration *Thinking skills: Analyze to identify figures of speech; classify the type of figurative language; compare figurative language to a possible replacement in literal language*	What figures of speech does the writer use? What do they accomplish that literal language would not?	Look throughout, but especially in descriptive passages, for various examples of figurative language and compare them to literal language.
Structure, including main sections and such organizational patterns as chronological order and order of importance *Thinking skills: Analyze to identify the sections of a text; classify to determine the organizational pattern*	What are the main sections of the text? What is the organizational pattern of the text?	Look throughout the text for transitional words and phrases that show both where sections break and how they are connected. Identify the main ideas from each section.
Point of view in fiction, including choice of narrator *Thinking skills: Analyze narrative to identify point of view; compare points of view by imagining a passage told from a different point of view and evaluating the effect.*	Is the story told from the first- or third-person point of view? If it is not in first-person, how much does the narrator know about the characters? What effect does the choice of narrative point of view have on the text? Why might the author have chosen that point of view?	Look for pronouns. If the narrator refers to himself or herself as "I," the story is in first-person. Look at key passages in which important information is revealed for examples that show the effect of point of view on the narrative.

continued

Focused Re-reading *(cont.)*		
Focus and Thinking Skills	**Questions to Ask**	**Finding Textual Evidence**
Point of view in nonfiction, including frame of reference, such as scientist, parent, teenager *Thinking skills: Recognize explicit statements; draw inferences about the writer from telling details*	What is the writer's frame of reference?	Look in the introduction and body paragraphs for details that give insight into the writer's experience, worldview, and possible bias.
Implied meanings *Thinking skills: Analyze details; draw inferences and conclusions*	What is left unsaid? What inference can you draw from a collection of details when you "read between the lines"?	Look throughout for details that "show" not "tell." In fiction these would include the actions of the characters and details of the setting. In nonfiction, these might appear in descriptive passages where the reader is left to draw his or her own conclusions. Find examples that support your interpretation of the implied meaning.

Different kinds of texts suggest additional points to focus on during re-reading.

Focused Re-Reading of Informational and Argumentative Text		
Focus and Thinking Skills	**Questions to Ask**	**Finding Textual Evidence**
Clarification and verification of information *Thinking skills: Define key terms; analyze complicated sentences and paragraphs; compare to other sources to verify information*	What parts confused you? What did you not understand well on first reading? What seemed to contradict information you thought you knew?	Look in passages that raised questions in your mind in first reading; refer to outside sources if necessary for confirming or contradicting information.
Assumptions *Thinking skills: Logical thinking to evaluate the assumption underlying the claim*	Does every claim depend on a valid assumption?	Look for passages that put forward claims in an argument; look for examples, if any, of hidden assumptions.

continued

Focused Re-Reading of Informational and Argumentative Text *(cont.)*		
Focus and Thinking Skills	**Questions to Ask**	**Finding Textual Evidence**
Development of an argument and key supporting ideas *Thinking skills: Evaluate the relevance, sufficiency, and importance of the supporting details; distinguish fact from opinion*	By what method does the writer attempt to prove his or her point? Are the supporting ideas relevant and sufficient to prove the point?	Look throughout for all the facts, reasons, and examples offered in support of each claim and/or counterclaim.
Style and tone *Thinking skills: Analyze language choices; evaluate appropriateness*	Is the style formal and respectful, or informal and full of "loaded" language (words that carry strong, usually negative connotations)?	Look throughout, but especially at the beginning and ending where the author wants to make his or her point most strongly, for examples that show formal, respectful language or disrespectful loaded language.

Focused Re-reading of Fiction and Drama		
Focus and Thinking Skills	**Questions to Ask**	**Finding Textual Evidence**
Plot *Thinking skills: Sequence; draw inferences; examine cause-effect relationships*	What is the impact of each main development of the plot on the characters?	Look for examples of characters' words or actions before a turning point in the story and after a turning point.
Setting *Thinking skills: Draw inferences*	How does the setting contribute to the mood of the story? How do the details of the setting help define characters?	Look for descriptive details throughout the story about the time and physical characteristics of the place of the events and their impact on mood and characters.
Characters *Thinking skills: Analyze details of characterization; generalize from details; draw inferences from details*	How does each character contribute to the development of the plot? How do the details of characterization and the dialogue reveal the characters' personalities and motivations? Why do characters act as they do?	Look throughout for character 1) descriptions, 2) thoughts, 3) words, 4) actions, 5) changes, 6) motivations.
Theme *Thinking skills: Draw inferences; generalize from details; synthesize various elements*	How does the author communicate the theme through the development of setting, characters, and plot? What passages and details in the story best express the main theme?	Look for passages and details from each main part of the story or drama that express theme.

Focused Re-reading of Poetry		
Focus and Thinking Skills	**Questions to Ask**	**Finding Textual Evidence**
Persona (the poet's "voice") *Thinking skills: Analyze; draw inferences*	How does the persona relate to the subject, mood, and theme of the poem?	Look for specific examples that show the persona's involvement and reveal attitudes.
Meter and rhyme *Thinking skills: Analyze meter and rhyme; synthesize to assess their effect*	How do the meter and rhyme affect the rhythm and mood of the poem?	Look for metrical patterns and rhyme schemes from several places in the poem.
Sound devices, such as alliteration, assonance, onomatopoeia *Thinking skills: Analyze language; classify types of sound devices; draw inferences about their meaning and effect*	What sound devices are in the poem? What effect do they have?	Look throughout the poem for examples of sound devices in relation to other elements of the poem.
Theme *Thinking skills: Draw inferences; generalize from details; synthesize various elements*	How does the poet communicate the theme through the details of the poem?	Look for passages and details from throughout the poem that express theme.

3. Synthesis: Evaluate the Text

By now you may have encountered the "new book" that close reading often reveals, a text with layers of meaning. On later re-readings, you can stand back from the text and begin to see it from a critic's point of view. Following are some of the criteria by which any great work of literature, or classic, is usually judged. When you evaluate a literary work, nonfiction or fiction, consider the following characteristics.

Some Characteristics of Great Literature
• Explores great themes in human nature and the human experience that many people can identify with—such as growing up, family life, personal struggles, or war
• Expresses universal values—such as truth or hope—to which people from many different backgrounds and cultures can relate
• Conveys a timeless message that remains true for many generations of readers
• Presents vivid impressions of characters, settings, and situations that many generations of readers can treasure
• Demonstrates outstanding and inventive understanding of important aspects of humanity and society

The chart below shows some questions you can ask—and answer with evidence from the text—when you are evaluating a text.

Questions for Evaluating a Text	
Informational Text	How effectively has the writer • presented a clear explanation on a topic of value • used examples and other supporting details • accurately conveyed information • structured the explanation • used language and style to add clarity and life • presented an unbiased view • engaged the reader
Argumentative Writing	How effectively has the writer • presented a clear position or claim on a subject of importance • used examples and other details to support claims • accurately conveyed information • addressed counterclaims • used logic • covered the topic in sufficient depth and breadth • been fair-minded • structured the argument • used language and style to add clarity and life • convinced you
Fiction and Drama	How effectively has the writer • drawn well-rounded characters worth getting to know • developed and paced a plot • set mood and tone • used language • structured the story • developed a meaningful theme
Poetry	How effectively has the poet • used (or not used) rhyme • created stunning word pictures • used figurative language • structured the poem • expressed an otherwise inexpressible idea

USING TEXTUAL EVIDENCE

Prove it! Anytime you write a literary analysis, informational text, or argument, you will be expected to prove your main idea or claim. You draw the **textual evidence** for that proof from the collection of details you have mined during your close readings.

During your close readings, you gathered evidence by taking notes from the work itself. These notes may have included descriptive passages, lines of dialogue, narrative details, facts, examples, statistics, and other kinds of details. In drafting an analysis of a text or in piecing together an informational or argumentative text from several sources, include the evidence in a way that will convince readers of your main idea or claim.

Strengthen your arguments by using relevant quotations from your text or texts that support a point. Work them smoothly into your writing and punctuate them correctly. The following guidelines show how to work textual evidence into a written analysis. They use examples from a literary analysis on a short story by Marjorie Kinnan Rawlings called "A Mother in Mannville."

Guidelines for Using Direct Quotations in a Literary Analysis

1. Always enclose direct quotations in quotation marks.
2. Follow the examples below when writing quotations in different positions in the sentence. Notice that quotations in the middle or end of a sentence are not ordinarily capitalized.

Begins Sentence	"He wore overalls and a torn shirt," observes the narrator (323).
Interrupts Sentence	In his "grave gray-blue eyes," the narrator sees a rare and precious quality (325).
Ends Sentence	The narrator feels that Jerry's integrity makes him "more than brave" (325).

3. Use ellipses—a series of three dots (. . .)—to show that words have been left out of a quotation.

    "For a moment, finding that he had a mother shocked me . . . and I did not know why it disturbed me" (327).
4. If the quotation is four lines or longer, set it off by itself without quotation marks. Indent one inch on the left and leave space above and below it.

> And after my first fury at her—we did not speak of
> her again—his having a mother, any sort at all, not far
> away, in Mannville, relieved me of the ache I had had
> about him. . . . He was not lonely. It was none of my
> concern. (328)

5. After each quotation cite the page number of the text in parentheses. The citation usually precedes punctuation marks such as periods, commas, colons, and semicolons. For plays or long poems, also give main divisions, such as the act and scene of the play or the part of the poem, plus line numbers.

Following are examples of using textual evidence in a different kind of writing—an informational research report on the lost city of Atlantis. The sources are indicated in parentheses and would be keyed to a works-cited page at the end of the report.

Examples of Using Textual Evidence in an Informational Report

1. Use a quotation to finish a sentence you have started.

   Example   Photographs taken in 1977 of underwater stones are believed to "bear the mark of human handiwork" (Whitney).

2. Quote a whole sentence. If you omit words from a sentence, indicate the omission with an ellipsis, a series of three dots (. . .).

   Example   "He suggests that the structures match the description in Plato's Dialogue Critias . . . and that the high mountains of Atlantis are actually those of the Sierra Morena and the Sierra Nevada" (Shermer).

3. Quote four or more lines from a source. For a quotation of this length, skip two lines and set the quotation as a block indented one inch on the left. You do not need quotation marks for such an extended quotation.

   Example   Here is how Plato describes the downfall of Atlantis in the dialogue called *Timaeus:*
   > Some time later excessively violent earthquakes and floods occurred, and after the onset of an unbearable day and a night, your entire warrior force sank below the earth all at once, and the Isle of Atlantis likewise sank below the sea and disappeared. (1232)

4. Quote just a few words.

   Example   According to Plato, in an "unbearable day and a night" Atlantis was destroyed (*Timaeus* 1232).

5. Paraphrase information from a source.

   Example   "Although many have dismissed Atlantis as a myth, some 50,000 volumes have been written to describe and locate it." [Original]
   Curiosity about Atlantis and efforts to locate it gave rise to some 50,000 books on the topic ("Greek Backs Plato Theory"). [paraphrase]

For informational and argumentative texts, including research reports, be sure to verify factual evidence in your sources for accuracy.

Verifying Factual Evidence

- Locate at least two sources that contain the same basic facts.
- Skim each source for specific details, such as dates, locations, and statistics.
- If the specific details in both sources agree, you can probably rely on their accuracy.
- Watch for discrepancies in broader concepts, such as in the sequence of events or in the relationship between cause and effect.
- If you discover discrepancies, use a third source to determine which source is likely to be more accurate.

COMPARING TEXTS

Another way to achieve a deep understanding of a text is to compare it to another text. You can compare and contrast literary texts in many ways. You could, for example, do a close reading of two (or more) texts using any of the same focus points outlined on pages 144–148, and then compare and contrast the way each text addresses that focus point. Following are just a few of many examples.

Two or More Texts of This Type	Focus Points to Compare and Contrast
Short stories	Structure (use of chronological order or flashbacks), theme, plot, character development, point of view, setting, style
Poems	Role of persona, figurative language, rhyme and meter, theme
Biographies	Details of life that are emphasized or omitted in each version; overall sense of person's character and motivation
Informational Texts	Structure, point of view, importance of main idea, support for main idea, language and style, author's purpose, accuracy of information, possible bias
Argumentative Texts	Structure, point of view, significance of main claim, quality of supporting details for claims, logical reasoning, accuracy of information, possible bias, language and style, conclusions

The following chart shows additional ways to compare and contrast texts to deepen your understanding of them.

Types of Texts to Compare	Questions for Comparing Texts
Texts in different forms or genres (such as stories and poems, historical novels and fantasy stories, short stories and novels)	• How is the approach to theme and topic similar in both forms? • How is the approach to theme and topic different in the two forms or genres? • How does their form or genre make these texts unique?
Fictional portrayal of a time, place, or character and a historical account of the same period	• How do authors of fiction use or alter history?
Modern work of fiction versus traditional sources	• In what ways does the modern work draw on themes, patterns of events, or character types from myths, traditional stories, or religious works? • How is the modern work turned into something new and fresh?

continued

Types of Texts to Compare *(cont.)*	Questions for Comparing Texts *(cont.)*
Texts from the same era that approach themes differently	• What was the purpose of each text? • What was the writer's frame of reference or worldview? • Whom was the writer addressing ?
Texts from different eras	• What does each text reveal about social attitudes during the time in which it was written?
Different texts by the same author	• What themes appear repeatedly in works by this author? • What changes in style and/or theme, if any, are apparent in later works by the author compared to earlier works?

Comparing Texts in Different Mediums "Texts" do not necessarily need to be written pieces. In fact, comparing texts in different mediums—such as print, audio, and video—can lead to valuable insights.

The following chart shows some questions to ask when comparing and contrasting texts in different mediums.

Reading a Story, Drama, or Poem	Listening to or Viewing an Audio, Video, or Live Version of the Text
• When you read the text, what do you see in your mind's eye? How do you picture the visual images, the characters, and the setting? • What do you hear—what do the characters' voices sound like? • What are the sounds in the setting? • What can you experience reading a text that you cannot experience when viewing or listening to an audio, video, or live version of the text?	• When you listen to an audio version of the text, what do you experience in comparison to when you read it? Are any elements more vivid? less vivid? • When you view a video version of the text, what do you experience in comparison to when you read it? • What can a video provide that a written text cannot? • How does the experience of a live performance differ from reading a text? • What can a live performance offer that reading a text cannot? • How faithful to the original text is the audio, video, or live version? If it differs in significant ways, why do you think the directors and actors made the choices they did to change it?

You know the techniques writers use to make an impression and impact. They include provocative language, narration that can get inside of characters' heads, and plenty of room for the readers' imaginations to fill in visual and auditory details. Understanding the "tools of the trade" of different mediums can help you make clear comparisons and contrasts.

Techniques of Audio	Techniques of Video	Techniques of Stage
• Actual voices and other sounds in the setting • Possibility of music to help create mood • Room for imagination to fill in visual aspects	• Representation of all sounds and visuals; little left to the imagination • Lighting, sound recording, camera angles, color, focus, and special effects all shape the visual message • Use of background music to help create mood • Editing techniques that place one scene next to another to make a comment	• Representation of some sounds and visuals within the limited scope of the stage • Stage directions that tell characters how to interact in each scene • Lighting and other special effects • Live actors creating a sense of immediacy • Use of music

Sometimes you may be asked to **compare a single scene in two different mediums.** For example, a chilling scene in the book *To Kill a Mockingbird* centers on the shooting of a mad dog by mild-mannered lawyer Atticus Finch. If you read that scene carefully in the book and then compared and contrasted it to the same scene in the movie version of the book, you could evaluate what is emphasized or absent in each treatment of the scene.

Sometimes you may be asked to **compare multiple versions of a story, drama, or poem in different mediums.** How does the stage version of *To Kill a Mockingbird* differ from both the print and movie versions? How do the film and stage versions offer different interpretations of the original text?

AUTHOR BIOGRAPHIES

MARGARET ATWOOD Born in Ottawa, Canada, where her father worked in the wilderness as an entomologist, Margaret Atwood spent much of her early life in the Canadian bush. She did not go to school full-time until she was eleven years old. Atwood got the hang of school, however, and earned a B.A. at the University of Toronto and an M.A. at Radcliffe College. She also did the coursework and reading for a Ph.D. at Harvard. Atwood published her first book, a collection of poems, at age nineteen. She describes her work, which has a realistic tone but blends both satire and fantasy, as speculative fiction. In addition to working as a writer, Atwood teaches writing and is politically active. She has taught and served as a writer in residence at many Canadian and American universities, and she is active in the PEN writers' group and in Amnesty International. Currently, she lives with her husband and daughter on a farm in Ontario.

OLIVIA E. COOLIDGE Born in London, England, in 1908, Olivia E. Coolidge studied Latin, Greek, and philosophy at Somerville College of Oxford University. A professional writer for 30 years, Coolidge used her love of ancient culture and language to retell mythological stories in a way that remains true to the past but alive in the present. In addition to retellings of mythology, she wrote the stories of major historical events such as the Trojan War and the Crusades. She also penned biographies of classical figures such as Alexander the Great, Lincoln, Gandhi, Churchill, Thomas Paine, and Eugene O'Neill.

BORDEN DEAL Growing up in a Mississippi farming family during the Great Depression, Borden Deal wanted to be a writer from the time he was six years old. As an adult, he wrote on his own time, after hours spent at jobs ranging from firefighter with the Civilian Conservation Corps to migrant wheat harvester. After serving in the Navy as an aviator cadet, Deal earned a B.A. in English and went on to do graduate work in Mexico City. While still in school, he published his first book. He continued writing in addition to earning a living until 1955, when he was able to become a full-time fiction writer. He published under his own name and under pseudonyms such as Lee Borden and Leigh Borden. Though he wrote on many subjects, he returned often to the themes of the land, identity, and ambition. His fiction is often strongly tied to the South and his characters often resemble the heroes of myths.

RITA DOVE As a child, Rita Dove saw her father break the race barrier in research chemistry. When she grew up, she began breaking down barriers in her own profession, writing. In 1970, she was recognized at the White House as one of the hundred most outstanding high school graduates in the United States. In 1973, she graduated *summa cum laude* from Miami University of Ohio and earned an M.F.A. from the University of Iowa. Dove spent two summers on Fulbright scholarships in Germany. She published her first book of poetry, *The Yellow House on the Corner*, in 1980. In 1987, she won the Pulitzer Prize for *Thomas and Beulah*, a book of poems about her grandparents. In 1993, she became the youngest person and the first African American to serve as poet laureate of the United States. In addition to poetry, Dove has written and published essays, stories, and a play that was performed in theatres around the world. She was poet laureate of the Commonwealth of Virginia from 2004–2006. She and her husband, the writer Fred Viebahn, have a grown daughter, Aviva Dove-Viebahn.

BERNARD EVSLIN Before he and his wife, Dorothy Evslin, began writing books for children in the 1960s, Bernard Evslin worked as a screenwriter and documentary film producer. Most of Evslin's books are about Greek mythology and history. He captured the bold bravado of Irish legend Finn McCool in *The Green Hero*, which was nominated for a National Book Award, and his exciting tale *Hercules* won the Washington Irving Children's Choice Award. Tom Evslin, the couple's son, describes his mother as "an author, teacher, and profile in courage." He calls his father, who died in 1993, "an author who made words sing."

NED HOOPES Although Ned Hoopes is an author, editor, and teacher in his own right, a summation of his life's work might well describe him as a writer who "plays well with others." Hoopes worked with Bernard and Dorothy Evslin and others on a variety of educational television and children's literature projects. He also edited anthologies of other people's work.

BETTY BONHAM LIES Not only an author and retired teacher, Betty Bonham Lies is a member of a loosely knit group of women who meet to critique each other's poems and perform them. An active member of the New Jersey Arts Council, Lies has written several prose works, including *Gallery Tales: Classical Mythology in the Art Museum* and *Earth's Daughters: Stories of Women in Classical Mythology*. Lies thinks myths are an important part of our human heritage because they communicate a society's moral and ethical values.

KATHLEEN LINES A British librarian and critic, Kathleen Lines is perhaps best known for her 1954 anthology entitled *Lavender's Blue: A Book of Nursery Rhyme*, a book that has never been out of print. Her ability to select and edit material has made her an important contributor to children's literature, from nursery rhymes to classical myths. Lines was born in 1902 and died in 1988.

BARBARA McBRIDE-SMITH claims she got her start as a storyteller when she heard wrong in class. When she was a child, a teacher told her the ancient Greeks lived in the cradle of western civilization. Barbara, who lived near Waco, Texas, imagined Zeus and his buddies as ancient cowboys. Her vivid and captivating mistake stuck with her, and when she became an adult, McBride-Smith transported several Greek myths and Biblical stories to contemporary times, often with hilarious results. McBride-Smith has developed an active form of storytelling she calls *story theatre*, which she both performs and teaches around the country. Her work has earned her the John Henry Faulk Award for Outstanding Contribution to Storytelling. She also has been inducted into the National Storytelling Network's Circle of Excellence.

GERALDINE McCAUGHREAN As a child, Geraldine McCaughrean wanted to do everything her older brother did. When he published a book, she decided she would do that too! McCaughrean was very shy as a child, and writing gave her a way to have adventures. When she grew up and got a job, she kept writing—on the way to work, on the way home, and on the weekends. In 1988, she devoted herself full-time to writing. Today, she has written more than 100 stories for children and adults. She has also written about 50 plays and a radio drama. Seven of her novels have won major children's book awards. And her work has been published in 25 languages. "Now," she says, "I stay home all day and write. It's great, but it still seems odd to earn a living by having so much fun."

SUNITI NAMJOSHI Born in Bombay, India, in 1941, as a young woman Suniti Namjoshi worked in the Indian civil service and academia for several years. She then moved to Montreal and attended McGill University, where she earned a Ph.D. in literature. Namjoshi taught at the University of Toronto for many years before accepting an appointment as a research fellow at the Centre for Women's Studies at Exeter University. Namjoshi's work touches on issues of gender, politics, and cultural traditions. Her works for children include retellings of Greek myths and studies of Greek culture, often with a feminist perspective.

ALDEN NOWLAN Born and raised in the Maritime of Windsor, Nova Scotia, Alden Nowlan wrote poetry that one critic lauded as a blend of "warm-heartedness and wry self-observation . . . a delicate balance of soul and spirit." Nowlan was mostly self-educated. He worked as a newspaperman and published poems, plays, short stories, and novels. Nowlan struggled with alcoholism most of his life and died at the age of 50 from pneumonia. He is remembered for producing simple and affecting work that embraces the lives of ordinary people.

LINDA PASTAN Poet Linda Pastan was born in New York in 1954. "By age ten or eleven," she says, "I knew I wanted to spend my life writing. But I don't think I knew that real people could be 'writers' until much later." Pastan has published numerous volumes of poetry, won countless prizes, and was named poet laureate of Maryland from 1991–1994. Exploring the themes of family, children, the passage of time, and the beauty of nature, Pastan manages to make everyday life worth writing—and reading—about. *The San Francisco Review of Books* describes her as "returning to the role of the poet as it served the human race for centuries: to fuel our thinking, show us our world in new ways, and to get us to feel more intensely about the ordinary."

HARRY MARK PETRAKIS Growing up poor but happy on Chicago's South Side during the Great Depression, Harry Mark Petrakis remembers his neighborhood as "a bazaar of nationalities: Irish, Polish, German, Italian, Greek . . . entwined in one another's lives." Petrakis began his writing career as a poet, but concentrated on writing stories after an experience at college in which fellow students refused to believe that one of his stories was fiction. For many years, Petrakis supported himself by making appearances at which he read and promoted his work. Sometimes, he traveled to two or more towns a day to read and talk about his work. Once his reputation was established, Petrakis slowed his appearance schedule, but he still writes full-time and lectures occasionally about the craft of writing.

PENELOPE PRODDOW A prolific translator, Penelope Proddow has translated or adapted Greek and Roman myths, Homeric hymns, and the Bible for children.

MICHAEL J. ROSEN Born and reared in Ohio, Michael J. Rosen still lives there with his family, which includes dogs and a cat. Rosen has always loved animals, especially dogs. He was a zoology major in college and has worked as a dog trainer. He also founded a grant program to help support animal humane societies. Rosen likes people too—and he likes to remind readers that people are also animals. He has received a lifetime achievement award for his work to fight hunger. In fact, Rosen writes primarily to bring attention to issues he cares about. "Humor is a salvation," he says.

W.H.D. ROUSE Born in 1863, W.H.D. Rouse became the headmaster of the Perse School in Cambridge, England, as an adult. He remained headmaster for 26 years. Rouse was known during his lifetime as an expert on Ancient Greece. He traveled frequently to Greece, studied classical literature, and taught both Greek and Latin as a spoken language. He also translated and published a collection of Latin and Greek songs, which he called "chanties." Rouse died in 1950.

ELLEN SWITZER and photographer Costas are frequent collaborators on nonfiction works for children. Their book *The Magic of Mozart: Mozart, the Magic Flute, and the Salzburg Marionettes* was nominated by the National Council of Teachers of English for an Obis Pictus award.

LOUIS UNTERMEYER was a major poet, writer, editor, anthologist, translator, and lecturer who never finished high school. He was born in New York City in 1885, and like many young men of his time, he quit school to work for his father as a jewelry manufacturer. Yet he couldn't resist writing. In 1911, Untermeyer published his first book of poems, *First Love*. Soon after, he and other left-leaning writers began publishing a Marxist journal, *The Masses*, which argued against U.S. involvement in World War I. After the U.S entered the war, the government forced the magazine out of business. Not to be deterred, Untermeyer and friends launched a new magazine called the *Liberator*. In 1923, Untermeyer quit working in his father's company and devoted himself full-time to literature. He continued working for leftist causes and during the McCarthy era was blacklisted. In 1956, however, he won a Gold Medal from the Poetry Society of America. Shortly afterward, he became a poetry consultant for the Library of Congress. Louis Untermeyer died in 1977.

ANNE TERRY WHITE Born in Ukraine (then part of Russia) in 1896, Anne Terry White came to live in the United States when she was eight years old. Her career as an author of materials for young people was born of a desire to help her two young daughters appreciate the world's great literature. She was a teacher, editor, and translator, as well as an author. White died in 1980.

ALISOUN WITTING Alisoun Witting worked as a reporter and photographer for the *Castine Patriot* in Maine. Her *Treasury of Greek Mythology* is a comprehensive collection of Greek myths.

RICHARD WOFF A historian who has written extensively about ancient Greece, Richard Woff has also written dictionaries of ancient Greek gods, goddesses, heroes, and heroines. He wrote a history of the ancient Olympics and published a book of stories that take place in ancient Greece. He also has written about the former Soviet Union.

JANE YOLEN Born in 1939 in New York City, Jane Yolen's parents moved the family to California before she was a year old. They returned to New York less than three years later. Yolen has published more than 150 books for children, and she has edited or contributed to hundreds more. In addition to retelling myths and fables, Yolen has created her own fairy tales, as well as other, more contemporary stories for young children, early readers, and older children. She is best known for her science-fiction and fantasy stories. Yolen is editor-in-chief of an imprint of fantasy literature for children and is a past president of SFWA (the Science Fiction and Fantasy writers of America). She also has taught literature and has served as a lecturer and critic.

ACKNOWLEDGMENTS

Text Credits CONTINUED FROM PAGE 2

"Demeter and Persephone" translated and adapted by Penelope Proddow. Doubleday & Company, Inc., Garden City, New York, 1972.

"Echo and Narcissus," courtesy of Golden Books Publishing Company, Inc. From *The Golden Treasury of Myths and Legends* adapted by Anne Terry White. © 1959, 1987 Golden Books Publishing Company, Inc. Used by permission. All rights reserved.

"The Firebringer" from *The Firebringer and Other Great Stories* © 1967, by Louis Untermeyer. Used by permission of the publisher, M. Evans and Company, New York.

"Look, Medusa!", by Suniti Namjoshi from *The Blue Donkey Fables*, London, Women's Press, 1988. Reprinted by permission of the author.

"I, Icarus" from *An Exchange of Gifts* by Alden Nowlan. Copyright © 1985 by Alden Nowlan. Reprinted by permission of Stoddart Publishing Co. Limited.

"Narcissus at 60", from *Carnival Evening: New and Selected Poems 1968–1998*, by Linda Pastan. Copyright © 1998 by Linda Pastan. Used by permission of W.W. Norton & Company, Inc.

"Pandora" from *Greek Myths, Western Style: Toga Tales with an Attitude* by Barbara McBride-Smith. © 1998 by Barbara McBride-Smith. Reprinted by permission of Marian Reiner.

"Perseus and Medusa" from *Bright Eyed Athena: Stories from Ancient Greece*, by Richard Woff. Copyright © Richard Woff 1999. Reprinted by permission of British Museum Press.

From "Pegasus for a Summer" by Michael Rosen from *When I Was Your Age, Vol. 2, Original Stories About Growing Up*,edited by Amy Ehrlich, Candlewick Press, 1999. Reprinted by permission.

"Persephone, Falling", from *Mother Love* by Rita Dove. Copyright © 1995 by Rita Dove. Used by permission of the author and W.W. Norton & Company, Inc.

"Phoenix Farm" by Jane Yolen. Copyright © 1996 by Jane Yolen, originally published in *Bruce Coville's Book of Magic*, published by Apple/Scholastic. Now appears in *Twelve Impossible Things Before Breakfast*, copyright © 1977 by Jane Yolen, published by Harcourt Brace.

"Siren Song" from *Selected Poems 1966–1984* by Margaret Atwood. Copyright © Margaret Atwood 1990. Reprinted by permission of Oxford University Press.

"A Whole Nation and a People" by Harry Mark Petrakis from *Reflections: A Writer's Life, A Writer's Work*, Lake View Press, Chicago, Illinois. Copyright © 1970 by Harry Mark Petrakis. Reprinted by permission of the author.

"The Wise Goddess: Athena" used with permission from *Earth's Daughters: Stories of Women in Classical Mythology* by Betty Bonham Lies. Copyright © 1999. Fulcrum Publishing, Inc., Golden Colorado. All rights reserved.

"Zeus and Hera" from *The Greek Gods* by Bernard Evslin, et al. Copyright © 1966 by Scholastic Inc. Reprinted by permission.

Every reasonable effort has been made to properly acknowledge ownership of all material used. Any omissions or mistakes are not intentional and, if brought to the publisher's attention, will be corrected in future editions.

Photo and Art Credits Pages 4–5: Corel. Pages 9–11: Erich Lessing/Art Resource, NY. Pages 12–13: www.arttoday.com. Page 17: © Cary Henrie. Page 18: Erich Lessing/Art Resource, NY. Page 22: Art Resource, NY. Page 25: © 2000 Ray Massey/Stone. Page 26: © Nostalgia/SIS. Page 30: © Phil Boatwright/SIS. Page 32: Private Collection/Bridgeman Art Library. Page 34: © Vanni Archive/CORBIS. Pages 34–35: Corel. Pages 40, 42, 45: RoxanaVilla.com. Page 47: © 2000 Chad Ehlers/Stone. Page 48: © Archivo Iconografico, S.A./CORBIS. Page 52: Alinari/Art Resource, NY. Page 56: Leeds Museums and Galleries (City Art Gallery) U.K./Bridgeman Art Library. Page 65: © 2000 Davies & Starr/Stone. Page 66: © 2000 Philippe Lardy c/o theispot™. Page 71: Tate Gallery, London/Art Resource, NY. © 2000 Foundation Gala-Salvador Dali / VEGAP / Artists Rights Society (ARS), New York. Page 73: © The Special Photographers Co./Photonica. Pages 74–75: Philadelphia Museum of Art: The George W. Elkins Collection. Page 79: Alinari/Art Resource NY. Page 83: Spencer Collection, Miriam and Ira D. Wallach Division of Art, Prints and Photographs, The New York Public Library, Astor, Lenox and Tilden Foundations. Page 84: Illustration by Nicholas Wilton. Page 92: Alinari/Art Resource, NY. Page 99: Scala/Art Resource, NY. Page 101: © Joan Hall. Page 102: © 2000 Eastcott/Momatiuk/Stone. Page 113: © Chris Hellier/CORBIS. Page 114: © 2000 Hulton Getty Picture Collection. Page 125: © Bettmann/CORBIS. Pages 126, 131: © Rodica Prato. Page 133: Louvre, Paris, France/Peter Willi/Bridgeman Art Library. Pages 134–135: © Giraudon/Art Resource, NY. Page 136: © Danny Bright/Photonica.